A CHECKLIST OF THE HOGARTH PRESS

Buff paper wrappers printed in red.
(See no. 16)

A CHECKLIST OF
THE HOGARTH PRESS
1917-1938

Compiled
by
J. Howard Woolmer

With a Short History
of the Press
by
Mary E. Gaither

1976
WOOLMER⁄BROTHERSON LTD
ANDES, NEW YORK

Published by
WOOLMER/BROTHERSON LTD
Gladstone Hollow
ANDES, NEW YORK
13731

Library of Congress Card Number: 75-7469

Printed in the United States of America

FOR BETTY & KEITH ROBERTSON

TABLE OF CONTENTS

LIST OF ILLUSTRATIONS

Photographs by Arden Ballantine

PREFACE

The checklist describes, to the best of my knowledge, every book and pamphlet published by The Hogarth Press from its inception in 1917 to the end of 1938, the year in which Virginia Woolf relinquished her interest. I have tried to personally examine at least one copy of each book, but in the few cases where this was impossible I have relied on descriptions provided by others. In only one instance has it been impossible to locate a copy of a book, Leonard Woolf's *Empire and Commerce in Africa* (no. 80), and this may yet turn out to be a Hogarth Ghost, that is, a book that was announced for publication or announced as published but which never appeared (the Ghosts are listed in the Appendix).

Entries are grouped under year of publication and then alphabetically by author. The month of publication and the number of copies printed are given for each entry when known, but this is not always possible because most of the records of the Press were destroyed during the blitz. The date on the title page determines the placement of each entry, even in cases where this differs from the actual publication date (for example, a book dated 1924 that was actually published in early 1925). I have used a number within parentheses to indicate the printer; a key to these numbers is supplied in the Appendix.

Descriptions of bindings and dust wrappers have been a great problem. In many cases these have faded so badly that it is difficult to determine the original shade; dust wrappers and labels that were originally white now appear to be cream. In cases where a book was printed and bound by the Woolfs paper for the wrappers was often purchased as needed, so that a variety of colors and patterns was used on the same title. For these reasons, it was decided to keep descriptions, particularly of colors, as simple as possible.

In cases where a book gives the appearance of having been issued in a dust wrapper, but where I haven't been able to locate a copy in dust wrapper, the statement "Dust wrapper not seen" is used. The number of pages given includes the last page of text plus index, if there is one, but does not include advertisements or blank pages.

The Uniform Edition of Virginia Woolf's works are not noted, nor are other reprints, except in cases where there is a specific reason for doing so. For example, each of the three printings of Norman Leys's *Kenya* (no. 48) has a new Preface, so each is noted; the first printing of E. M. Forster's *Pharos and Pharillon* (no. 29) was hand-printed by the Woolfs, but the later printings were done commercially. Catalogues of Hogarth Press publications and ephemeral advertising leaflets have not been listed.

Compilers of bibliographies and checklists are always hopeful that they haven't missed anything, and I am no exception. As a bookseller, however, I've been using these tools long enough to know how difficult completeness is to achieve. All I can ask is that I will be told about any omissions or any errors I have made.

The checklist could never have been compiled without the help of a great many individuals. If I have left anyone out of the following list, it's entirely accidental, and does not lessen my appreciation. Robert Brotherson; Andreas Brown (Gotham Book Mart); John Byrne (Bertram Rota Ltd); William R. Cagle, Geneva Warner, and the staff of The Lilly Library, Indiana University; Alan Clodd; Mrs. Louis Henry Cohn (House of Books, Ltd.); Dr. David Farmer, Assistant Director, Humanities Research Center, The University of Texas; Prof. Mary E. Gaither; Donald Gallup; Angelica Garnett for permission to reproduce covers by Vanessa Bell; K. C. Gay, Curator of Poetry Collections, State University of N.Y. at Buffalo; Harcourt Brace Jovanovich, Inc. for permission to quote from Leonard Woolf's *Beginning Again* and *Downhill All The Way* and Virginia Woolf's *A Writer's Diary*; Carolyn Harris; Peter Howard (Serendipity Books); B. J. Kirkpatrick for the information gleaned from her Bibliographies of E. M. Forster and Virginia Woolf; David Koch, Rare Book Librarian, Southern Illinois University, Carbondale; George Lawson (Bertram Rota Ltd); Jean Peters; Prof. S. P. Rosenbaum, University of Toronto; George Rylands for permission to quote from a letter to Mary Gaither; George A. Spater for assistance at the very beginning of my labors and for reading proofs and supplying further information at the end; Dr. Lola Szladits of the Berg Collection and Peter Rainey of the Rare Book Division of the New York Public Library.

J. Howard Woolmer

Introduction

THE HOGARTH PRESS: 1917-1938

MARY E. GAITHER

WITHOUT the imprimatur of Leonard and Virginia Woolf
it is likely that The Hogarth Press would have attracted
little attention from students of literature or bibliophiles.
The Press, a small concern and originally without ambition
to be more than a hobby for its founders, entered the
commercial lists almost in spite of itself. The fame it has
achieved has been the result of its very close identification
with its owners and their conception and influence: because
the Press was small it was also personal both in the re-
flection of the views its publications expressed and in the
selection of the authors it published. Both owners were
writers and critics of note with wide and overlapping circles
of social and professional acquaintances. It sometimes hap-
pens that a small, independent publisher holding to high
and exacting standards of intellectual content and aesthetic
form, with only a secondary concern for profit making
(that is to say that although he does not especially want
to *make* money, at the same time, understandably, he does
not want to *lose* any), earns a secure reputation for publishing books that voice the foremost literary, social, and
political ideas of the day, a reputation that may go beyond
even that enjoyed by larger and older houses. Such publishers were Leonard and Virginia Woolf at The Hogarth
Press.

The present Hogarth Press has been an allied company
of Chatto and Windus since 1947 and as such will not be
considered here. Rather the focus is on the Press as founded
and developed by the Woolfs from 1917 to 1938 when
Virginia withdrew as a partner and John Lehmann became
part-owner with Leonard. From its amateur beginning in

the dining room of the Woolf home in Richmond through its removal to larger quarters in London and to the onset of World War II, there is a consistent insistence upon intellectual and artistic worth that helps to explain why the Press became a self-supporting business and a significant publishing voice in England between the wars. Some measure of this significance and worth, in the area of literature in particular, can be taken by reference to the ANNALS OF ENGLISH LITERATURE, 1475-1950: from 1921, when Virginia's *Monday or Tuesday* appeared in the ANNALS as the first Hogarth title, through 1938 there were thirty-three Hogarth titles listed, at least one every year except 1936 and as many as three in 1927, 1929, and 1931 and four in 1925 and 1938. There can be no doubt that the Woolfs, launching series after series dealing with psychoanalysis, art and literary criticism, poetry, politics, and social affairs, felt, as did Sir Stanley Unwin, that publishing afforded "a wide scope for initiative" and provided "endless opportunities to help the cause of progress."[1]   Two of the most obvious illustrations of the Woolfs' initiative are their publishing the first translations into English of now acknowledged masterpieces from contemporary foreign literatures, and the important papers of the International Pyscho-Analytical Institute at Vienna. The cause of progress for the Woolfs meant, in part, publishing enlightened and clear thinking from well-informed persons on such vital and controversial issues as disarmament, the League of Nations, imperialism, racial prejudice, educational reform, labor conditions, socialism, etc. It also meant the encouragement of little-known and unknown poets and novelists who were breaking away from traditional patterns and creating new forms to express new views and new ways of looking at old problems: they published early poems of T. S. Eliot as well as *The Waste Land*, works by Katherine Mansfield, Robert Graves, C. Day Lewis, William Plomer, Christopher Isherwood, and, of course,

[1] *The Truth about Publishing* (London: Allen and Unwin, 1950), p. 332.

those of Virginia Woolf herself. To a very satisfying degree The Hogarth Press was in the vanguard in publishing new writers and fresh ideas, and the circumstances that brought about their activity make an interesting chapter in English cultural history.

The Hogarth Press deliberately remained a small operation, a part-time activity of its owners. Leonard admits that "one reason why the Press survived was because for many years our object was, not to expand, but to keep it small."[2] From the first single booklet published in 1917 through the seventeen titles published in 1938, the Press published a total of 440 titles, including the pamphlets and little essays in the various series. Although its output was small,[3] its contribution to significant intellectual thought and literary trends of the 1920s and 1930s was exceptionally high. To glance at the list of Hogarth authors is to recognize one prominent name after another. In addition to those mentioned above, the list includes, for example, Clive Bell, G. D. H. Cole, E. M. Forster, Roger Fry, John Maynard Keynes, Harold Laski, F. L. Lucas, Rose Macaulay, Allardyce Nicoll, Harold Nicolson, V. Sackville-West, and H. G. Wells.

As publishers, two people as active as the Woolfs in the literary, political, and intellectual foreground of their time were bound to attract the interest of their professional associates and friends, and The Hogarth Press list reflects this attraction and their common interests. Cambridge, Bloomsbury, *The Nation*, the Labor Party, the Fabian Society, all are represented in the list, and most of what is presented is good. Leonard himself comments particularly on

---

[2] *Beginning Again* (London: Hogarth Press, 1964), p. 255. Subsequent references to this edition will appear in the text as *BA*.

[3] How small, but how increasingly solvent, can be judged by the income it earned the Woolfs from 1924 through 1938: from a low of £3 in 1924 to highs of £2,373 in 1931 and £2,442 in 1938. Yet in 1934, 1935, and 1936 its earnings were only £930, £741, and £637, respectivley. The average annual income it returned its owners during this fifteen-year period was £814. See Leonard Woolf, *Downhill All the Way* (London: Hogarth Press, 1967), p. 142. Subsequent references to this edition will appear in the text as *DATW*.

the interaction of his position as literary editor of *The Nation* and as publisher trying to find and to help new authors:

> All sorts of literary fish, some the same as and some different from the *Nation's* shoals, swam in and out of the Hogarth Press in Tavistock Square. It was possible to help the budding (and sometimes impecunious) Hogarth author by giving him books to review and articles to write; and, if one came across something by a completely unknown writer which seemed to have something in it, one could try him out with articles and reviews before encouraging him to write a book. Thus Tom Eliot, Virginia, E. M. Forster, Robert Graves, Vita Sackville-West, William Plomer came to the *Nation* via the Press, while Edwin Muir was an example of the reverse process in this shuttle service. (*DATW*, p. 130)

And undoubtedly Henry Brailsford, Philip Noel-Baker, Charles Buxton, and Arther Ponsonby came to the Press because of Leonard's political associations and *The Political Quarterly*. Yet it must not be forgotten that the Woolfs set out deliberately to publish what they wanted--and never what they did not want.[4] This policy did not change even after they became commercial publishers. The Press's independence and individuality were evident from its earliest beginnings.

❦ ❦ ❦

Leonard Woolf and Virginia Stephen met at Cambridge when Virginia and her older sister Vanessa (later Mrs. Clive Bell), "the beautiful Stephen sisters," would come to to visit their brother Thoby at Trinity and stay with their cousin Miss Katherine Stephen, Principal of Newnham. Thoby, Leonard, Lytton Strachey, Clive Bell, Saxon Sydney-Turner, and John Maynard Keynes formed a very

---

[4] Interview with Leonard Woolf, 30 May 1961. See also *Beginning Again*: "...one would have to refuse absolutely, as we did for many years, to publish anything unless we thought it worth publishing or the author worth publishing" (p. 255).

closely knit social and intellectual group that came under the influence of G. E. Moore, the philosopher, Fellow of Trinity. The so-called Bloomsbury Group, which was to include also E. M. Forster, Roger Fry, and Desmond McCarthy, had its roots here among these friends at Trinity. After going down from Cambridge, Leonard went to Ceylon as a Civil Servant in 1904, resigning when he returned on leave in 1911. He and Virginia were married in 1912, moved to Richmond in October 1914, and then to Tavistock Square, London in 1924.

As the daughter of Sir Leslie Stephen, author, editor of *Cornhill Magazine* and editor of and contributor to *The Dictionary of National Biography*, Virginia had family and social connections that included many prominent names such as Thackeray, Duckworth, and Maitland. Her literary career as one of the significant figures of the first third of the century brought her in touch with many writers and critics of varying talents and reputations. Leonard was a writer, too, and an editor, an active Fabian Socialist, and a working member of the Labour Party. In 1913 he published his first book, a novel, *The Village in the Jungle*, in 1916 *International Government*, and *Empire and Commerce in Africa* in 1920. He was literary editor of *The Nation* from 1923 to 1930. In this latter year, with Professor William A. Robson, he started *The Political Quarterly*, becoming its editor in 1932, a position he held until 1959, becoming then its literary editor. Between 1919 and 1945 he worked for the Labour Party as secretary of two Advisory Committees, and from 1938 to 1955 he was a member of the National Whitley Council for Administrative and Legal Departments of the Civil Service. Among his other books are *Essays on Literature, History, Politics, etc.* (1927); *After the Deluge: A Study in Communal Psychology*, Vol. I (1931), Vol. II (1939), and Vol. III, *Principia Politica* (1951); *The Hotel*, a play (1939).

The establishment of The Hogarth Press grew quite simply out of the Woolfs' interest in printing, an interest that Leonard capitalized upon to give Virginia an ideal

form of relaxation when the pressures of writing threaten-
ed to destroy her mental equilibrium. And it provided
them both with a hobby.

Early in 1917 the Woolfs applied for admission to the
St. Bride Foundation Institute in Bride Lane, Fleet Street,
headquarters of the London Society of Compositors, to
learn the art of printing. Because they did not intend to
become members of the printers' trade union they were
denied admission. But they were not easily daunted. Walking later in Farringdon Road nearby they visited a printing
shop, The Excelsior Printing Supply Co., where they bought
a small handpress, complete with instruction booklet, and
some Old Face type for £19.5s.5d. They set the press up
in their dining room at Hogarth House in Paradise Road,
Richmond, hence the name Hogarth Press.[5]

After teaching themselves the rudiments of printing,
they began printing their first publication in May, the first
of a total of thirty-four to be hand-set and printed by them.
This hand-sewn, paper-covered booklet, published in July
"casually and without consideration," according to the
Foreword to the *Complete Catalogue of Publications* issued by
The Hogarth Press in 1939, was *Two Stories* written by themselves: "Three Jews" by Leonard and "The Mark on the
Wall" by Virginia. It is an unprepossessing little pamphlet
of thirty-one pages bound in Japanese grass paper, some
in dull blue, some in an over-all red and white design.[6]
There are four woodcuts by Dora Carrington, for which

---

[5] In 1915, three years after their marriage, the Woolfs had moved
into Hogarth House as renters. Built in the early eighteenth century,
it had originally been one large country house, but in the nineteenth
century it had been divided, one half being named Hogarth House,
the other, Suffield House. It has today been joined as one and is
owned and partly occupied by the Richmond and Barnes Conserva-
tive Association. A bridge club and local businessmen are the other
occupants.

[6] B. J. Kirkpatrick, in *A Bibliography of Virginia Woolf*, 2nd rev. ed.
(London: Rupert Hart–Davis, 1967), lists a third cover, "thin yellow
paper wrappers," and adds, "Mr. Leonard Woolf states that paper
for the wrappers was purchased as wanted from a local stationer.
It is therefore possible that the work was issued in other coloured
wrappers" (p. 7).

she was paid fifteen shillings (*BA*, p. 237). By the end of the month they had sold for 1s 6d each 124 copies of the 150 they had printed (*BA*, p. 236).

The Woolfs decided that if *Two Stories* succeeded, they would "print and publish in the same way poems or other short works which the commercial publisher would not look at" (*BA*, p. 235). Announcing its publication, they invited people to buy their little book of stories. Leonard records that 134 copies were sold and that among the purchasers, all except "five or six of them friends or acquaintances," were Arthur Ponsonby and Charles Trevelyan, both M.P.s, Mrs. Bernard Shaw and Mrs. Sidney Webb (*BA*, p. 236). The total cost of the production was £3.7s.0d. and the total receipts £10.8s.0d (*BA*, p. 237). Subsequent publications were not to be so informally sold. Describing their plans for printing and publishing, they invited people to become subscribers to Hogarth publications by one of two plans: Plan A, all publications would automatically be sent to the subscriber; or Plan B, the subscriber would be notified of each publication as it appeared and given the opportunity to accept or decline it. There were "eventually" forty-five A subscribers and forty-three B subscribers (*BA*, p. 236). From the sole-surviving account book of the Press, that for 1920-1922, we learn that among the subscribers were Katherine Murry (Mansfield), Logan Pearsall Smith, Duncan Grant, Roger Fry, John Maynard Keynes, Hope Mirrlees, Lytton Strachey, Mrs. Harold Nicolson (V. Sackville-West), Lady Ottoline Morrell, and Hugh Walpole.[7] They continued to sell their books on this subscription basis until 1923, when, finding their business had grown so, they changed to the more orthodox manner of sales and distribution by selling to booksellers at a discount.

Encouraged and pleased by the success of their first publication, the Woolfs embarked upon a more ambitious project: they printed and published in 1918 a sixty-

[7] See Stanley B. Olson, "The History of the Hogarth Press: 1917-1923," Diss. University of London 1972, Appendix C.

eight page story which its author had offered them in response to their informal request, *Prelude* by Katherine Mansfield. Virginia set most of the type for this story while Leonard did all the machining. But it was a bigger job than their press could handle, so they finally resorted to borrowing larger chases from a nearby job printer, McDermott, and using his press which could print four crown octavo pages at a time. They printed 300 copies of *Prelude* and bound it in plain, dark blue paper wrappers and sold it for 3s.6d. A very few copies were first bound in blue wrappers with block designs by the Scottish painter J. D. Fergusson, but these designs were soon abandoned because the Woolfs disliked them.[8]

Also in 1918 they printed and published a second book for private distribution, and it deserves a mention because of its personal connection with the Woolfs. *Poems* by Cecil N. Sidney Woolf, Leonard's younger brother, who was killed in action in France in 1917, was a memorial volume containing seventeen poems written between 1909 and 1914.

Four more books were added to their list in 1919. Three of them—T. S. Eliot's *Poems*, Virginia Woolf's *Kew Gardens*, and Hope Mirrlees's *Paris*—were hand-printed; the fourth one, John Middleton Murry's *Critic in Judgment*, was printed for them, but they did the binding themselves. Although the date on the title page of *Paris* does indeed read 1919, it did not actually come out until 1920. Unlike the other volumes they hand-printed, the imprint here reads "Printed by Leonard and Virginia Woolf," not "Printed and published by Leonard and Virginia Woolf" as became standard.

Eliot's *Poems* contains seven poems, "vintage Eliot" as Leonard described them: "Sweeney among the Nightingales," "The Hippopotamus," "Mr. Eliot's Sunday Morning Service," "Whispers of Immortality," "Le spectateur" (since changed to "Le directeur"), "Mélange adultère de tout," and "Lune de miel." Its publication marked a "red letter

---

[8] See Katherine Mansfield to John Middleton Murry and Katherine Mansfield to Virginia Woolf, *The Letters of Katherine Mansfield*, ed. J. Middleton Murry (New York: Knopf, 1932), pp. 162-163.

day" for the Press and the Woolfs and the beginning of a long and respected friendship with "Tom" Eliot (*BA*, pp. 242-245). Their acceptance of these poems is one of many illustrations of Leonard's contention that they were dedicated to publishing only what they wanted, never what they did not want. They published Eliot's *Poems* and *The Waste Land* (1923) simply because they thought they were good poems.[9] Leonard records his own immense satisfaction in setting the type for these poems in contrast to the irritation he felt at the monotonous repetition of other works as page after page came from the press:

> But I never tired and still do not tire of those lines which were a new note in poetry and came from the heart of the Eliot of those days (and sounded with even greater depth and volume in the next work of his which we published, the poem which had greater influence upon English poetry, indeed upon English literature, than any other in the 20th century, *The Waste Land*) . . . (*BA*, p. 243).

Fewer than 250 copies of *Poems* were printed. Published in May and selling for 2s.6d., it was out of print by the middle of 1920 and was not reprinted.

Reviewers of early Hogarth publications were often put off by their appearance—the bright paper wrappers—and sometimes by their content. This early unenthusiastic response is evident in a combined review of the Eliot and Murry pieces, which appeared in *The Times Literary Supplement* for 12 June 1919 under the title "Not Here, O Apollo." As the title suggests, the review is not favorable to either poet. Murry is accused of trying to say so much so easily one cannot discover what it is he is saying, whereas Eliot is accused of the opposite, of writing verse that is novel, ingenious, and original, but "impoverished by subject matter." The reviewer concludes that

> The final effect of these two little books is to leave us all the more melancholy because of the authors'

[9] Interview with Leonard Woolf, 30 May 1961.

cleverness. If they were nothing, it would not matter;
but they are something, and they are very laboriously
writing nothing (p. 322).

The review has held up in its assessment of Murry's poem,
but time has shown there to have been a certain shortsight-
edness in Eliot's case.

The most dramatic factor in the Woolfs' becoming significant commercial publishers was their printing and publishing of Virginia's *Kew Gardens*. It was the unexpected and
unprepared-for demand for this short story, bound in col-
ored wrappers and illustrated with woodcuts by her sister,
Vanessa Bell, that sent the Woolfs to a commercial printer
for help to fill the orders that poured in. They themselves
had printed only 150 copies; they ordered a second edition
of 500 copies from the printer, Richard Madley. The cause
of this sudden demand was a very favorable review which
appeared in the *TLS* on 29 May 1919. When they published
Kew Gardens on May 12 they sent a review copy to the *TLS*,
and until the review appeared they had sold only 49 copies.
Virginia tells the exciting story of the effects of the review
in *A Writer's Diary* (London: Hogarth Press, 1953):

> ...we came back from Asheham [June 3] to find the
> hall table stacked, littered with orders for *Kew Gardens*.
> They strewed the sofa and we opened them intermit-
> tently through dinner, ... we were both excited ....
> All these orders—150 about from shops and private
> people—come from a review in the *Lit. Sup.* presumably
> by Logan [Pearsall Smith], in which as much praise
> was allowed me as I like to claim (p. 15).

The review reads in part:

> But here is "Kew Gardens"—a work of art, made,
> "created" as we say, finished, four-square; a thing of
> original and therefore strange beauty, with its own
> "atmosphere," its own vital force. Quotation cannot
> present its beauty, or as we should like to say, its be-
> ing, ... Perhaps the beginning might be suppler; but
> the more one gloats over "Kew Gardens" the more
> beauty shines out of it; and the fitter to it seems this

cover that is like no other cover, and carries associations; and the more one likes Mrs. Bell's "Kew Gardens" woodcuts (p. 293).

The cover admired so by the reviewer was the first of several such covers for which the Press became known. They were of heavy paper, some of wallpaper, very colorful, some made by Roger Fry and his daughter, others imported. This particular one is dark brown with marbled splotches of bright blue and rust. Speaking in general of these paper covers Leonard wrote:

> For many years we gave much time and care to finding beautiful, uncommon, and sometimes cheerful paper for binding our books, and, as the first publishers to do this I think we started a fashion which many of the regular, old established publishers followed. We got papers from all over the place, including some brilliantly patterned from Czechoslovakia, and we also had some marbled covers made for us by Roger Fry's daughter in Paris (BA, p. 236).

This second edition of Kew Gardens was sold out by the end of 1920 and was not reprinted. The story was included in Virginia's Monday or Tuesday, a collection of her short stories which the Press published, but did not print, in 1921. Six years later, in 1927, they issued a special limited edition of 500 copies of Kew Gardens, printed on the recto leaf only and decorated by Vanessa Bell, printed and engraved by the printer, Herbert Reiach.

The full significance of the commercial printing of the second edition of Kew Gardens is summed up simply by Leonard: "We found ourselves in the publishing business almost in spite of ourselves."[10] However, it took more than this one success alone to set them firmly on the path to becoming more than just amateur printers and publishers. The next move, which was to be even more decisive, was their publishing in 1920, in addition to two hand-printed books, two works that were too long for them to print

[10] Interview, 30 May 1961.

themselves: Maxim Gorky's *Reminiscences of Leo Nicolayevitch Tolstoi* (71 pp.) and Logan Pearsall Smith's *Stories From the Old Testament* (53 pp.). There were to be no repeats of the *Prelude* experience. These were composed and printed for them commercially by the Pelican Press which had printed the second edition of Virginia's *The Mark on the Wall* (1919). The Gorky volume, published in July, sold out in a few months and was reprinted before the end of the year and issued in January 1921. The publishing of these two books, as pointed out in the Foreword of the Press's 1939 catalogue, "almost unintentionally, turned the Press into a regular publishing business. . . . From that moment the Press continually received the offer of books which it was impossible for them to print themselves and some of which were so good they did not like to refuse them." These two volumes have another significance: they exemplify two kinds of books for which the Press was to gain recognition. First, original translations of notable works from foreign literatures which the press could claim responsibility for bringing to the English reading public for the first time—selected works from Bunin, Tolstoi, Rilke, and Italo Svevo, for example—were published at fairly regular intervals. Of the twenty-nine translations published between 1920 and 1938, exclusive of the titles in the International Psycho-Analytical Library, only one had ever before been published in English—*The Diary of Montaigne's Journey to Italy* (1903). The Woolfs took a personal interest in these translations, even to the point of collaborating, each separately, with S. S. Koteliansky in individual translations from Bunin, Tolstoi, Gorky, and Dostoevsky. Second, the Press was receptive to publishing unorthodox interpretations of tradition and biographies of little-known but interesting personalities. Smith's *Stories from the Old Testament* was a retelling and reinterpretation of some Biblical incidents that attempt to see more clearly into the minds of some Old Testament worthies and "to arrive at a more historical and just appreciation of the causes and motives of their actions" (p. 5). To some readers the reinterpretations might seem irreverent; to others they are a fresh and illuminating view.

In the space of four years, with nine separate titles and three reprints to its credit, The Hogarth Press had gradually became an established business. In 1921, they published Virginia's *Monday or Tuesday* (hand-set, but printed by McDermott with Leonard's help and anguish), Leonard's *Stories of the East*, Clive Bell's *Poems*, both the latter handprinted, and another translation by Koteliansky and Leonard of Tchekhov's *Note-books*, together with *Reminiscences of Tchekhov* by Maxim Gorky, commercially printed. It must be remembered that there had been almost no capital investment as such in the founding of the business. The only financial outlay was for the press and the type; the investment of the two owners' time, labor, and talent was gratis; and because the Press was in their own home, there was no overhead for rent. Their costs were for paper and other materials, hired labor, and royalties to other authors. In these early days, what they made on their publications they put back into the operation. But they were expanding, and in 1921 they bought another printing press, a Minerva, for £70.10s.0d. and seventy-seven pounds of 12pt. Caslon Old Face type for £18.9s.5d. By 1923 they had invested a total of 135 2s 3d in the Press for printing presses, type, and materials (*DATW*, p. 72).

Because the Press had become a growing concern, its editorial and managerial activities and responsibilities began to be a bigger job than the two owners wished to handle alone, particularly as they still wanted the Press to be only a part-time activity. They considered themselves primarily writers, not publishers. For a short time in 1918 they had been assisted by Barbara Hiles (later Bagenal) who had worked chiefly on *Prelude*, but she soon left. It became apparent that if they wished to continue to operate the Press while still maintaining their writing careers they must have some regular help. Toward this end they hired near the end of 1920 Ralph Partridge as a part-time assistant; he remained with them until March 1923. But part-time help proved to be only a stopgap. The pressures and demands of the whole publishing business, aggravated by the Woolfs' having been unprepared for handling the enterprise they almost literally and unwittingly found themselves the parents of, and the unsatisfactoriness of depending on only part-time help forced the Woolfs in late 1922 to face squarely the decision of whether to continue the Press or not. Leonard comments candidly on the situation:

> . . . we were already committed to publish full-length, important books, not only for Virginia herself, but also for writers whom we considered important. We felt to these writers and their books the responsibility of the commercial publisher to the author, we had to publish their books professionally and competently . . . . We found ourselves sitting uncomfortably on the horns of a dilemma—and the same situation would build itself up again and again from time to time over the following years. Shall we give up the Press altogether or shall we make one more attempt to find a manager or a partner who will help us to run this commercial hippogriff on the lines which we want it to develop? We were then . . . very much inclined to give the whole thing up and leave ourselves free of responsibility to pursue our other activities. On the other hand, we were urged from the outside to develop the Press and naturally were rather flattered by this (*DATW*, pp. 78-79).

Quite unexpectedly they found the interested full-time person they needed, and this discovery helped them to resolve their dilemma. They accepted neither the offer of James Whittall, "a cultured American," to become a partner nor that of the publisher Heinemann to take the Press into a kind of partnership. Instead they hired in January 1923 Mrs. Marjorie Thomson Joad, a former teacher who had become interested in printing and publishing, at a salary of £100 per annum and a half of the share of the profits. She remained with them for two years, accompanying them when they moved to London in 1924.

In addition to Mrs. Joad, other assistants at the Press were, in particular, George (Dadie) Rylands, Angus Davidson, and John Lehmann. George Rylands was with the Press "for a few months (from the summer of 1924, I think) as an apprentice who might perhaps become more involved in the concern."[11] At the time, he was writing his fellowship dissertation for King's College, Cambridge, and finally gave up his job at the Press to devote all his time to his writing. His description of his activities at the Press gives a rare picture of the kind of life and intimacy that friends enjoyed with the Woolfs, even as they worked:

> In the basement in Tavistock Square . . . I had many happy hours setting up type with Virginia and helping Leonard with the hand press (or battling inkily and unsuccessfully with it on my own)—doing up parcels, selling books to travelers—meeting their friends—listening and talking about literature . . . . They were very flattering in asking my views but I was very young, straight from College, . . . fortunately CRITICISM had not been INVENTED then, so we talked and argued. The Woolfs were very encouraging about my dissertation—Indeed they not only published it as *Words and Poetry* with a preface by Lytton Strachey but also printed a little book of my verses.

After Rylands came Angus Davidson, who remained with the Press from December 1924 to the end of 1927. Davidson was a friend of Rylands at Cambridge and it was initially through Rylands that both Davidson and, later, John Lehmann became associated with the Press. When Davidson left, he was succeeded by a Richard Kennedy, who engagingly records his impressions of his two years there in a recent volume entitled *A Boy at the Hogarth Press* (London: Whittington, 1972). John Lehmann came in 1931.

Of all these assistants, Lehmann was the most dedicated, the most interested in publishing, and the most influential

---

[11] Letter to the author, 29 June 1965.

in his job.[12] He took an active part in seeking new authors—Christopher Isherwood, for instance—and he undoubtedly gave poetry a special impetus. *New Signatures* (1932),
the "manifesto" of the new poets of the 1930s, owes much
to him. He was connected with the Press at two different
times. The first association was a relatively brief one, as
apprentice-manager, for just over a year from early 1931
to the autumn of 1932. He returned six years later, in
1938, as part-owner and general manager, and remained
until 1946 when Leonard bought out his interest.[13] In 1939,
The Hogarth Press printed *A Complete Catalogue of Publications
Arranged Under Subjects. To the Summer of 1939.* In its "Foreword" it was announced that Leonard Woolf and John Lehmann were the sole partners, "but on literary questions they
have the benefit of the advice of the following distinguish-
ed authors: W. H. Auden, Christopher Isherwood, Rosamond Lehmann, V. Sackville-West, Stephen Spender, and
Virginia Woolf."

It is true that the running of the Press in Richmond was
fairly amateurish. Having installed the Minerva press in
the larder because it was too heavy for the dining room,
the Woolfs printed there, bound in the dining room, and
wrapped for mailing and interviewed printers, binders, and
authors in the sitting room. This homey arrangement was
to change with their removal to London. The Woolfs had
taken a five-year lease on Hogarth House when they moved
there in 1915, and in 1920 had bought the entire property
including Suffield House, with the thought of remaining
there. But the inconvenience of the location with the in-
creased business of the Press, the Woolfs' increasing social
engagements in London, and Virginia's growing sense of
isolation living in Richmond away from theatres, art

[12] He started his own publishing firm after he left The Hogarth
Press in 1946. A poet and founder and editor of *New World Writing* and
editor of *The London Magazine* until 1961, he is now President of the
Royal Literature Fund.

[13] For his detailed accounts of both these experiences see *The
Whispering Gallery* (London: Longmans, Green, 1955), pp. 164-194 and
the whole of *I Am My Brother* (London: Longmans, Green, 1960).

galleries, concert halls, and close friends, all supported their decision to move to London. In March 1924 they moved into 52 Tavistock Square, on which they took a 10-year lease. The ground and first floors were already occupied by a legal firm, Dollman and Pritchard. The Press was housed in the basement and the Woolfs occupied the second and third floors. With the Press now in separate quarters of its own and with a full-time assistant, the Woolfs settled down to accepting the fact that they had become full-fledged publishers.

Although they were to continue hand-printing books as a hobby, as their publication lists gradually grew they became commercial publishers depending upon commercial printers. Over the years they were to employ the services of a number of printers, but Clark of Edinburgh and the Garden City Press of Letchford were the ones they did the most business with and with whom very cordial and personal relations were established. Leonard speaks warmly of Clark's representative, William Maxwell, in describing Maxwell's keen and professional interest in their "strange, unorthodox venture into printing." He would usually find time to come out to Richmond, while they were still there, to visit the Press whenever he came to London. His personal interest was reflected in the same care that he took with a job for 1,000 copies as with one for 20,000 (*DATW*, p. 73). And it was the Garden City Press that gave The Hogarth Press a home during the war after it had been bombed out in Mecklenburgh Square, where the Woolfs had moved in 1939.[14]

To return to the publications of the Press. The year 1924 marked another turning point. In addition to moving from Richmond to London, a major decision in itself, the Press assumed the publication of the papers of the International Psycho-Analytical Institute, as a result of which it later became the authorized publisher of the works of Freud. In the short space of seven years, the Press had been able to so establish a reputation for initiative, energy,

[14] Lehmann, *I Am My Brother*, pp. 85-86.

and reliability that it could be approached for such a major undertaking.

After Dr. Ernest Jones, psychoanalyst and ardent disciple of Freud, helped establish a branch of the Institute of Psycho-Analysis in London, he wanted to have the papers of the Vienna-based Institute translated into English and distributed in England. Arrangements were made with an English publisher for the publication and distribution of the papers as they came out in Vienna, and the first one appeared in 1921. These papers were under the general editorship of Dr. Jones, assisted by James Strachey (brother of Lytton), psychoanalyst and translator. But in 1924, after the first six numbers had appeared, negotiations for the publication of the papers of the International Psycho-Analytical Library, as they were called, were made with The Hogarth Press. The Press added these first six numbers to its list, of which two were works by Freud, *Beyond the Pleasure Principle* and *Group Psychology and the Analysis of the Ego*, and in 1924 published Numbers 7 and 8 (Volumes I and II of Sigmund Freud's *Collected Papers*). Leonard accepted the publication and distribution upon the condition that the Press would have the power of veto on all future publications. The papers appeared on a regular basis until the end of 1938, numbering thirty-one in all, and included six more works by Freud. They appeared under the imprint of The Hogarth Press and The Institute of Psycho-Analysis. The success of this venture was such that Leonard was encouraged to publish a standard edition of Freud in English. The first volume of *The Standard Edition of the Complete Psychological Works of Sigmund Freud* appeared in 1953, the last in 1966, a total 24 volumes. They were translated under the general editorship of James Strachey in collaboration with Anna Freud. The importance of the International Psycho-Analytical Library material is seen in the practical perspective of paper allowances during the war. John Lehmann describes the paper ration for the Press as being so small that priorities had to be observed for war-time publications. Virginia's titles in the Uniform Edition and

Freud's works in the International Psycho-Analytical Library (there were ever-increasing requests from America for the Freud material) were given first consideration along with reprints in urgent demand. Very little was left over for new titles.[15] And from the vantage point of forty years, Leonard in 1961 saw the opportunity presented to him to publish the International Psycho-Analytical Library as "rather fortuitous."

Now firmly settled in London, with its reputation becoming wider because of the Gorky translations, Virginia's *Jacob's Room* (1922) and *Mrs. Dalloway* (1925), and the publications of the International Psycho-Analytical Institute, The Hogarth Press truly became established as a respected publisher. Its publications lists grew longer and included a wider scope of subjects. Within seven years after its first publication the annual list had grown from one to twenty titles and had branched out to include art, travel, biography, literary and art criticism, psychoanalysis, and foreign affairs, in addition to the fiction and poetry the Woolfs had published during their first three years. This list continued to increase until it reached a peak of thirty-six titles in 1932, falling off to twenty in 1933, then rising slightly to twenty-one and twenty-four in the next two years, declining to seventeen by 1938. The production of the Press was obviously and indiscriminately affected by the general and worldwide depression that began in 1930 and by the onset of World War II. But the subjects published continued to grow in variety and significance: domestic issues—economics, trade, government, labor, education, finance—political theory, disarmament, aesthetics, religion, music criticism and music history, and even etiquette and health.

One of the distinctive features of the Press is the several series on a number of different subjects that it initiated. All the titles in these series were specifically commissioned or sought out, and because all the numbers, except for the Lectures on Literature, were short and

15 *I Am My Brother*, p. 153.

published as pamphlets, the Press was able to offer to the
general reading public attractive, inexpensive booklets containing brief but usually provocative statements by such
well-known persons as T. S. Eliot, John Maynard Keynes,
Roger Fry, Harold Laski, and Robert Graves, that might
otherwise not have been written. All the series were con-
ceived of as a way, deliberately, to bring before the public
significant ideas in literature, art, politics, and criticism.
Some of the series were more successful than others, The
Hogarth Essays and the Day to Day Pamphlets, for instance; one was so unsuccessful it was discontinued, The
Hogarth Letters.

The first series that the Woolfs published was The
Hogarth Essays, First Series, 1924-1926, nineteen titles.
This was followed by a Second Series, 1926-1928, sixteen
titles. These sold for an average of 2s.6d. and were from
twenty to sixty pages in length. They deal chiefly with
literature and literary criticism, with an occasional number
on aesthetics or politics. The Hogarth Lectures on Literature,
First Series, 1927-1931, contains fifteen titles[16]; Second Series, 1934, only one. These are books rather than pamphlets,
running to an average of 160 pages, and sold for 3s.6d.
The Hogarth Living Poets, First Series, 1928-1932, twenty-
four volumes; Second Series, 1933-1937, five volumes, differ
from the other series in that they are collections of original poems rather than essays or discussions. They were
published under the general editorship and sponsorship
of Dorothy Wellesley (Dorothy Violet Wellesley, Duchess
of Wellington). The Day to Day Pamphlets, 1930-1939,
forty titles, 1s.6d. each, is a series dealing with contemporary social, political, and economic issues. Readers of this
series were presented brief, generally lucid, liberal, often
left-wing, views that were intended to inform, provoke
thought, and challenge opinion. It was for this series that
the Press device of a highly stylized wolf head was designed

---

[16] This series was resumed in 1951 under the editorship of George
Rylands.

by E. McKnight Kauffer.[17] The Hogarth Letters, 1931-1932, twelve issues, were familiar little essays on a variety of topics: new poetry, new novels, the state of the church, what it means to be an Englishman, childhood and growing up, Hitler, etc. It is a pity that they were not better received, for aside from the Day to Day Pamphlets, these letters contain some of the liveliest and most convincing statements in any of the series. Except for one, they were published as an omnibus volume in 1933. A series of short biographies called World Makers and World Shakers, 1937, issued only four titles which deal with Socrates, Joan of Arc, Darwin, and Mazzini, Garibaldi, and Cavour. A last series, not falling within the time limits of this list, The Hogarth Sixpenny Pamphlets, 1939, is of sufficient interest to warrant listing the authors and titles of the five numbers: E. M. Forster, *What I Believe*, Stephen Spender, *The New Realism*, John Betjeman, *Antiquarian Prejudice*, Virginia Woolf, *Reviewing*, and Graham Bell, *The Artist and His Public*.

A number of individual titles in the various series became little classics in their own right and sold extremely well, for example, F. L. Lucas's *Tragedy in relation to Aristotle's Poetics* (Lectures on Literature, 1927), Maurice Dobb's *Russia Today and Tomorrow* (Day to Day Pamphlets, 1930), and *New Signatures*, edited by Michael Roberts (Hogarth Living Poets, 1932, 1934).

In sum, the books and pamphlets published by The Hogarth Press from 1917 through 1938 make an impressive list by any standard. There is a heavy emphasis on literature and the inclusion of the names of two major artists of the twentieth century is the crown: T. S. Eliot (his early work) and Virginia Woolf (all of her work after the first two novels). But this does not minimize the importance of Katherine Mansfield, E. M. Forster, Robert Graves, William Plomer, C. Day Lewis, and Christopher Isherwood

---

[17] The more representational wolf head in a medallion used earlier as the device of the Press was designed by Vanessa Bell and first appeared, in a larger size than elsewhere, on the title page of Virginia Woolf's *The Common Reader* (1925).

on the list. The omission of the name of James Joyce is in no wise the failure of the Woolfs to recognize him. In 1918, Eliot introduced to the Woolfs Miss Harriet Weaver of *The Egoist*, which had published "The Love Song of J. Alfred Prufrock." She gave them the manuscript of Joyce's *Ulysses* to consider for publication. They read it and decided that they would like to publish it; however, they were unable to find a printer who would accept the job, for fear of prosecution, and so were forced finally to return the manuscript to Miss Weaver. Even D. H. Lawrence appears on the list, albeit by the back door, perhaps--his name is listed as one of the translators, with Koteliansky and L. Woolf, of Bunin's *The Gentleman from San Francisco* (1922). The entire list, especially after 1924, reflects some of the most significant contemporary thought as it dwelt on the main issues of the day. In addition, the hand-printed volumes of poetry and fiction, the translations from foreign literature, and the papers of the International Psycho-Analytical Library each contributes to The Hogarth Press a special stamp. Finally, one must not lose sight of the achievement of the Woolfs' original intention—as they innocently embarked upon the publishing venture that eventually brought them fame and a moderate income—to publish unlikely works that might not be published elsewhere.

DEVICES OF THE HOGARTH PRESS

Designed by Vanessa Bell

Designed by E. McKnight Kauffer

Publications

TWO STORIES

HOGARTH PRESS
RICHMOND

Paper-backed red-and-white cloth printed in black.

1 9 1 7

1. Woolf, Virginia & L. S. *Two Stories* Written and Printed by Virginia and L. S. Woolf Hogarth Press Richmond 1917
§ Japanese paper or paper-backed cloth printed in black (see note).
31 pp. (1) $8\frac{7}{8}$ x $5\frac{5}{8}$.
Published July 1917; 150 copies printed.
NOTE: "Publication No. 1" appears at head of title page.
Because the material for the wrappers was bought as needed it varies from paper-backed cloth in a red-and-white geometric design (see illustration) to plain blue paper-backed cloth to plain yellow paper.
Contains *Three Jews* by Leonard Woolf and *The Mark on the Wall* by Virginia Woolf.

1 9 1 8

2. Mansfield, Katherine *Prelude* Hogarth Press Richmond.
§ Blue paper wrappers printed in black.
68 pp. (1) $8\frac{1}{2}$ x 6.
Published May 1918; 300 copies printed.
NOTE: A few copies, number not known, were issued with a line block by J. D. Fergusson on the blue wrapper. The block had been selected by Katherine Mansfield, but Virginia Woolf didn't like it and it was dropped.
On the last page of the text is stated "Printed by Leonard and Virginia Woolf at the Hogarth Press." The book was printed by the Woolfs, but at their friend McDermott's THE PROMPT PRESS, not on their own handpress.

3. Woolf, C. N. Sidney   *Poems by C. N. Sidney Woolf*
Hogarth Press, Richmond
§ White paper wrappers printed in black.
Unpaginated (but 19 pp.) (1) $5\frac{3}{8}$ x $4\frac{1}{4}$.
Publication date and number of copies printed not known.
NOTE: Poems by Leonard Woolf's brother who was killed in World War I. Printed for private circulation. There is a note in the copy at the Lilly Library: "Only this copy and the one in the British Museum are known to have survived." Undoubtedly the rarest of all Hogarth Press publications, but I suspect that there are more than two copies in existence.

POEMS
T. S. ELIOT

POEMS
T. S. ELIOT

4. **Eliot, T. S.** *Poems* Printed & published by L. & V. Woolf at The Hogarth Press, Hogarth House, Richmond 1919

§ Paper wrappers; label printed in red or black (see note).

13 pp. (1) $9\frac{1}{4}$ x $6\frac{1}{8}$.

Published May 1919; fewer than 250 copies printed.

NOTE: Earliest copies were bound in paper wrappers of varying texture and design with a label printed in red (see illustration of a copy bound in same material as *Two Stories* [no. 1]). Later copies were bound in marbled paper wrappers, the majority with a label printed in black.

5. **Mirrlees, Hope** *Paris a Poem* Printed by Leonard & Virginia Woolf at The Hogarth Press, Paradise Road, Richmond 1919 (1920)

§ Paper wrappers with a gold, blue, and red diamond design; white label printed in red.

23 pp. (1) 6 x $4\frac{1}{2}$.

Published May 1920; 175 copies printed.

NOTE: The poem is dated "Spring 1916" on page 22, but this has been changed to "1919" in ink in all the copies I've seen.

6. **Murry, J. Middleton** *The Critic in Judgment or Belshazzar of Baronscourt* Hogarth Press, Hogarth House, Richmond

§ Black paper wrappers; white label printed in black.

26 pp. (11) $9\frac{1}{4}$ x 6.

Published June 1919; 200 copies printed.

NOTE: Printed by THE PROMPT PRESS, Richmond, but bound by the Woolfs.

7. **Woolf, Virginia** *Kew Gardens* Hogarth Press Richmond 1919

§ Paper wrappers hand-colored in blue, brown, and orange on a black ground; white label printed in black.

16 pp. (1) size varies from 9 x $5\frac{7}{8}$ to $9\frac{3}{8}$ x $5\frac{7}{8}$.

Published May 1919; 150 copies printed.

NOTE: On page 16, the statement "Printed by Leonard & Virginia at The Hogarth Press, Richmond" is changed by a cancel-slip to "L. and V. Woolf."

The woodcut appears in three states: (1) printed on the page, (2) printed on a separate piece of paper and pasted onto the page, and (3) printed on a separate piece of paper and pastsd over original.

8. **Woolf, Virginia** *The Mark on the Wall* Second Edition Hogarth Press, Richmond 1919 (taken from upper cover; issued without a title page)

§ White paper wrappers printed in black.

10 pp. (10) $8\frac{3}{8}$ x $5\frac{1}{2}$.

Published June 1919; 1,000 copies printed.

NOTE: First separate edition; first appeared in *Two Stories* (see No. 1).

1 9 2 0

9. **Forster, E. M.** *The Story of the Siren* Printed by Leonard & Virginia Woolf at The Hogarth Press, Paradise Road, Richmond 1920

§ Blue marbled paper wrappers; white label printed in black (see note).

14 pp. (1) $9\frac{1}{2}$ x $5\frac{3}{4}$.

Published July 1920; 500 copies printed.

NOTE: Also bound in green, grey, and orange marbled paper wrappers. The label appears in at least three states: (*a*) label edged in gold, $1\frac{7}{8}$ x $4\frac{1}{8}$, printed in black within a triple frame in gold: *The Story of the* | *Siren* | *E. M. Forster*; (*b*) as above, but: *The Story* | *of the Siren* | *E. M. Forster*; (*c*) plain white label, 1 to $1\frac{5}{8}$ x $2\frac{3}{4}$ or 1 x $3\frac{3}{4}$, printed in black: *The Story of the Siren* | *E. M. Forster*.

10. **Gorky, Maxim** *Reminiscences of Leo Nicolayevitch Tolstoi* Authorized Translation from the Russian by S. S. Koteliansky and Leonard Woolf. Published by Leonard & Virginia Woolf at The Hogarth Press, Paradise Road, Richmond 1920

§ Green marbled paper wrappers; white label printed in black.

71 pp. (10) $7\frac{1}{4}$ x 5.

Published July 1920; 1,000 copies printed.

NOTE: A second edition bound in purple paper wrappers printed in black was published in January 1921 but dated 1920. The title page gives no indication that it is a second edition, but it contains a "Translators' Note to Second Edition" and a few notes not included in the 1920 edition.

11. **Smith, Logan Pearsall** *Stories From the Old Testament Retold by Logan Pearsall Smith* The Hogarth Press Richmond 1920
§ Blue paper wrappers; white label printed in black.
53 pp. (10) $7\frac{1}{4}$ x $4\frac{3}{4}$.
Publication date and number of copies printed not known.

1 9 2 1

12. **Bell, Clive** *Poems* Printed & published by Leonard and. Virginia Woolf at the Hogarth Press, Richmond, Surrey. 1921
§ Stiff buff paper wrappers, lettered and with a clover design in red on front cover.
29 pp. (1) 8 x $5\frac{1}{4}$.
Published December 1921; 350 copies printed.

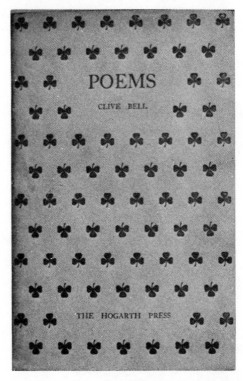

First impression

13. **Fry, Roger** *Twelve Original Woodcuts* Printed and Published by Leonard and Virginia Woolf at The Hogarth Press Hogarth House Richmond 1921
§ Marbled paper wrappers decorated by hand in various colors; white label printed in black.
Unpaginated, 12 plates (1) 9 x 6½.
Published December 1921; number of copies printed not known.

NOTE: Went into at least three impressions. I haven't seen a copy of the second impression, but the third impression was also printed by the Woolfs, in 1922, and bound in buff paper wrappers with the twelfth woodcut reproduced on the top cover. It was printed on coated paper without the titles to the woodcuts, otherwise it was identical to the first impression.
Referred to in Leonard Woolf's *Downhill all the Way* (The Hogarth Press 1967) under the title "Woodcuts."

14. **Gorky, Maxim** *The Note-Books of Anton Tchekhov Together with Reminiscences of Tchekhov* Translated by S. S. Koteliansky and Leonard Woolf. Published by Leonard & Virginia Woolf at The Hogarth Press, Paradise Road, Richmond 1921
§ Red marbled paper boards; white label printed in black.
108 pp. (12) 7¼ x 4⅞.
Publication date and number of copies printed not known.
NOTE: Also issued in blue paper boards.

15. **Prewett, Frank** *Poems* (The following appears on the verso of the title page: Printed & Published | For the Author | at | The Hogarth Press | Richmond)
§ Coated white paper wrappers printed in black.
Unpaginated (1) 8⅞ x 5¾.
Published August 1921; number of copies printed not known.

16. **Woolf, Leonard** *Stories of the East* Printed and published by Leonard and Virginia Woolf at the Hogarth Press, Hogarth House, Richmond 1921
§ Buff paper wrappers printed in red.
55 pp. (1) 8 x 4⅞.
Published April 1921; 300 copies printed.

17. **Woolf, Virginia** *Monday or Tuesday* With Woodcuts by Vanessa Bell Published by Leonard & Virginia Woolf at The Hogarth Press, Hogarth House, Richmond 1921 § White paper boards printed in black; brown cloth spine. 91 pp. (11) $7\frac{3}{8}$ x $4\frac{7}{8}$.

Published March 1921; 1,000 copies printed.

NOTE: Hand-set and printed by McDermott (with Leonard's help) at THE PROMPT PRESS, Richmond.

1 9 2 2

18. **Andreev, Leonid** *The Dark* Translated by L. A. Magnus and K. Walter 1922 (1923) Published by Leonard and Virginia Woolf at The Hogarth Press, Hogarth House, Richmond § White paper wrappers printed in black. 52 pp. (15) $8\frac{3}{8}$ x 6.

Published January 1923; number of copies printed not known.

19. **Bunin, I. A.** *The Gentleman From San Francisco and other stories* Translated from the Russian by S. S. Koteliansky and Leonard Woolf. Published by Leonard & Virginia Woolf at The Hogarth Press, Paradise Road, Richmond 1922 § Paper boards decorated in blue, green, and yellow; white paper labels on top cover and spine printed in black. 86 pp. (12) $7\frac{1}{4}$ x $4\frac{3}{4}$.

Published May 1922; about 1,000 copies printed.

NOTE: Errata slip pasted to title page stating that the first story was translated by D. H. Lawrence and S. S. Koteliansky and that Lawrence's name had been omitted in error.
Announced under "Forthcoming Publications" in Ruth Manning-Sander's *Karn* (No. 14) under the title "Four Short Stories."

20. **Dostoevsky, F. M.** *Stavrogin's Confession and The Plan of the Life of a Great Sinner* With Introductory and Explanatory Notes. Translated by S. S. Koteliansky and Virginia Woolf. Published by Leonard & Virginia Woolf at The Hogarth Press, Paradise Road, Richmond 1922

§ White paper boards printed in ice-blue, ice-blue cloth spine; white labels printed in black on spine and cover. Kirkpatrick's *Bibliography of Virginia Woolf* mentions a wax paper dust wrapper. (See note.)

169 pp. (2) $7\frac{1}{2}$ x 5.

Published October 1922; about 1,000 copies printed.

NOTE: There is a secondary binding of ice-blue cloth with white paper label printed in black on spine.

21. **Freud, Sigm(und)** *Beyond the Pleasure Principle* Authorized Translation from the Second German Edition by C. J. M Hubback. The International Psycho-Analytical Press London Vienna MCMXXII

THE INTERNATIONAL PSYCHO-ANALYTICAL LIBRARY NO. 4.

§ Green cloth printed in gilt. **Blue-green dust wrapper printed in black.**

90 pp. (26) $9\frac{1}{2}$ x $6\frac{1}{4}$.

Published October 1922; number of copies printed not known.

NOTE: The first volume in The International Psycho-Analytical Library to be published by The Hogarth Press. The Hogarth imprint doesn't appear on the title page, but it does appear on the top cover and dust wrapper.

22. **Freud, Sigmund** *Group Psychology and the Analysis of the Ego* Authorized Translation by James Strachey. The International Psycho-Analytical Press London, Vienna, 1922.

THE INTERNATIONAL PSYCHO-ANALYTICAL LIBRARY NO. 6.

§ Green cloth printed in gilt. Dust wrapper not seen.

134 pp. (28) $9\frac{3}{8}$ x $6\frac{1}{8}$.

Published December 1922; number of copies printed not known.

NOTE: The Hogarth imprint appears on the top cover and dust wrapper only.

23. **Manning-Sanders, Ruth** *Karn* Printed and Published by Leonard and Virginia Woolf at The Hogarth Press Hogarth House Richmond 1922

§ Gold paper boards; red label printed in black.

45 pp. (1) $8\frac{1}{2}$ x $5\frac{1}{2}$.

Published May 1922; 200 copies printed.

24. Shove, Fredegond *Daybreak* Printed and published by Leonard and Virginia Woolf at The Hogarth Press, Hogarth House, Richmond. 1922
§ White paper boards decorated in various colors; white label printed in black.
43 pp. (1) $7\frac{1}{4} \times 5\frac{1}{4}$.
Published May 1922; 250 copies printed.
NOTE: Errata slip loosely inserted.

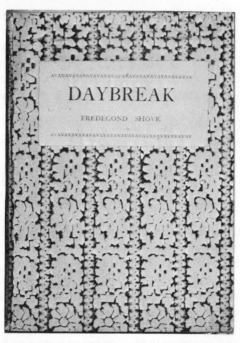

25. Tolstoi, Countess Sophie *The Autobiography of Countess Sophie Tolstoi* With Preface and Notes by Vasilii Spiridonov. Translated by S. S. Koteliansky and Leonard Woolf. Published by Leonard & Virginia Woolf at The Hogarth Press, Paradise Road, Richmond 1922
§ Paper boards decorated in blue and yellow; white labels printed in black on spine and top cover.
126 pp. (12) $7\frac{3}{8} \times 4\frac{7}{8}$.
Published June 1922; 1,000 copies printed.
NOTE: Listed under the title "The Autobiography of Tolstoi's Wife" in the advertisements in Fredegond Shove's *Daybreak*.

26. **Woolf, Virginia** *Jacob's Room* Published by Leonard & Virginia Woolf at The Hogarth Press, Hogarth House, Richmond 1922

§ Yellow cloth boards; white label printed in black on spine. Cream dust wrapper printed in cinnamon and black.

290 pp. (2) $7\frac{1}{2}$ x 5.

Published October 1922; 1,200 copies printed.

NOTE: There were also forty copies issued for "A" subscribers with printed slip signed by the author tipped in on the front endpaper.

1 9 2 3

27. **Bell, Clive** *The Legend of Monte della Sibilla or Le Paradis de la Reine Sibille* Printed and Published by Leonard and Virginia Woolf at The Hogarth Press   Hogarth House Richmond 1923

§ White paper boards printed in black. White dust wrapper printed in black.

25 pp. (1) $10\frac{1}{4}$ x 7.

Published December 1923; 400 copies printed.

NOTE: "With decorations and a cover design by Duncan Grant and Vanessa Bell" printed on dust wrapper.

28. **Eliot, T. S.** *The Waste Land* Printed and published by Leonard and Virginia Woolf at The Hogarth Press Hogarth House Paradise Road Richmond Surrey 1923 § Blue marbled paper boards; white label printed in black (see note).

35 pp. (1) 9 x 5$\frac{1}{2}$.

Published September 1923; about 460 copies printed.

NOTE: The label appears in three states: with a border of asterisks, with a single rule above and below the title, and without rules. The size of the label varies for each state.

29. **Forster, E. M.** *Pharos and Pharillon* Printed and Published by Leonard and Virginia Woolf at The Hogarth Press Hogarth House Paradise Road Richmond Surrey 1923 § White paper boards printed in Cambridge blue shot through with royal blue, bright blue cloth spine; white label printed in black (see note).

80 pp. (1) 8$\frac{3}{4}$ x 5$\frac{5}{8}$.

Published May 1923; 900 copies printed.

NOTE: Covers appear in two states: with the royal blue design running horizontally or with it running vertically.
The book varies in size from 8$\frac{1}{2}$ x 5$\frac{1}{2}$ to 8$\frac{3}{4}$ x 5$\frac{5}{8}$.
Reprinted several times; the reprints were done commercially by R. & R. Clark.

30. **Fry, Roger** *A Sampler of Castile* Published by Leonard and Virginia Woolf Hogarth Press Richmond 1923
§ Dull white paper boards, grey cloth spine, printed in black. Cream dust wrapper printed in purple.
75 pp. plus 16 plates (2) $11\frac{3}{4}$ x 9.
Published November 1923; limited to 550 numbered copies.

31. **Fry, Roger** *Duncan Grant* With an Introduction by Roger Fry. Published by Leonard & Virginia Woolf at The Hogarth Press, Paradise Road, Richmond 1923 (1924)
§ Quarter ivory cloth on ivory paper boards printed in black. Dust wrapper not seen.
9 pp. plus 24 plates (2) 10 x $7\frac{5}{8}$.
Published February 1924; number of copies printed not known.
NOTE: *Living Painters—Duncan Grant* appears on the half-title.

32. **Goldenveizer, A. B.** *Talks with Tolstoi* Translated by S. S. Koteliansky and Virginia Woolf. Published by Leonard & Virginia Woolf at The Hogarth Press, Paradise Road, Richmond 1923
§ Pink marbled paper boards, buff cloth spine; white label on spine printed in black. Wax paper dust wrapper.
182 pp. (2) $7\frac{5}{8}$ x 5.
Published June 1923; about 1,000 copies printed.

33. **Graves, Robert** *The Feather Bed* With a cover design by William Nicholson. Printed and Published by Leonard & Virginia Woolf at The Hogarth Press Hogarth House Richmond 1923
§ Pink paper boards, black spine, printed in black and white.
28 pp. (1) $9\frac{7}{8}$ x $6\frac{7}{8}$.
Published July 1923; limited to 250 numbered and signed copies.
NOTE: Contains an "Introductory Letter to John Ransome (sic), the American Poet."

34. **Jones, Ernest** *Essays in Applied Psycho-Analysis* The International Psycho-Analytical Press, London, Vienna, 1923
THE INTERNATIONAL PSYCHO-ANALYTICAL LIBRARY NO. 5.
§ Green cloth printed in gilt. Dust wrapper not seen.
454 pp. (26) $9\frac{1}{4}$ x 6.
Published October 1923; number of copies printed not known.

35. **Limebeer, Ena** *To a Proud Phantom* Printed and Published by Leonard and Virginia Woolf at The Hogarth Press Richmond 1923 (1924)
§ Multicolored marbled paper boards, white label printed in black.
32 pp. (1) $7\frac{5}{8}$ x $5\frac{1}{8}$.
Published July 1924; 250 copies printed.

36. **Lowther, Alice** *When it was June* Published by Leonard & Virginia Woolf at The Hogarth Press, Richmond 1923
§ Blue cloth; white label on spine printed in black. Cream dust wrapper printed in black.
84 pp. (2) $7\frac{1}{2}$ x $4\frac{3}{4}$.
Published November 1923; number of copies not known.

37. **Luce, G. H.** *Poems* New Edition with Decorations by Duncan Grant. Published by Leonard and Virginia Woolf at The Hogarth Press Hogarth House Paradise Road Richmond Surrey 1923 (1924)
§ Paper boards marbled in black, blue, purple, etc.; white label on spine printed in black.
54 pp. (2) 9 x $5\frac{5}{8}$,
Published February 1924; number of copies printed not known.
NOTE: First published by Macmillan in 1920.

38. **Read, Herbert** *Mutations of the Phoenix* Printed and Published by Leonard & Virginia Woolf at The Hogarth Press Hogarth House Richmond 1923
§ Red marbled paper boards, red cloth spine; white label on spine printed in black.
51 pp. (1) $9\frac{7}{8}$ x $7\frac{3}{8}$.
Published May 1923; 200 copies printed.

39. **Reynolds, Stephen** *Letters* Edited by Harold Wright.
Published by Leonard & Virginia Woolf at The Hogarth
Press, Paradise Road, Richmond 1923
§ Blue cloth printed in gilt. Wax paper dust wrapper.
346 pp. (2) $9\frac{1}{4}$ x $5\frac{3}{4}$.
Published May 1923; number of copies not known.

40. **Tolstoi, (Leo N.)** *Tolstoi's Love Letters with a study of the
autobiographical elements in Tolstoi's work, by Paul Biryukov*
Translated from the Russian by S. S. Koteliansky and
VirginiaWoolf. Published by Leonard & Virginia Woolf
at The Hogarth Press, Paradise Road, Richmond 1923
§ White paper boards printed in red and green, green
cloth spine; white label on spine printed in black. Wax
paper dust wrapper (see note).
134 pp. (2) $7\frac{5}{8}$ x 5.
Published May 1923; about 1,000 copies printed.
NOTE: There is a second binding in green cloth; white label on
spine printed in black.

1 9 2 4

41. **Avvakum** *The Life of the Archpriest Avvakum by Himself*
Translated from the Seventeenth Century Russian by
Jane Harrison and Hope Mirrlees, with a Preface by
Prince D. S. Mirsky. Published by Leonard and Virginia
Woolf at The Hogarth Press, 52 Tavistock Square, Lond-
on, W.C. 1924
§ Blue and black mottled cloth; white label on spine print-
ed in blue. Dust wrapper not seen.
156 pp. (2) $6\frac{7}{8}$ x $4\frac{1}{8}$.
Published November 1924; number of copies not known.

42. **Bosanquet Theodora** *Henry James at Work* Printed and
published by Leonard and Virginia Woolf at The Hogarth Press, 52 Tavistock Square, London. 1924
THE HOGARTH ESSAYS, FIRST SERIES, NO. 3
§ Cream paper wrappers printed in green.
33 pp. (1) $8\frac{3}{8}$ x $5\frac{1}{2}$.
Published November 1924; number of copies not known.
NOTE: This is the only book in The Hogarth Essays Series to be
hand-printed by the Woolfs.

43. **Eliot, T. S.** *Homage to John Dryden Three Essays on Poetry of the Seventeenth Century* Published by Leonard and Virginia Woolf at The Hogarth Press, Tavistock Square London, W.C.1 1924

THE HOGARTH ESSAYS, FIRST SERIES, NO. 4

§ Cream paper wrappers printed in black.

46 pp. (8) $8\frac{1}{2}$ x $5\frac{1}{2}$.

Published November 1924; about 2,000 copies printed.

44. **Freud, Sigm(und)** *Collected Papers* [4 volumes] Authorized Translation under the supervision of Joan Riviere. The International Psycho-Analytical Press   New York London Vienna MCMXXIV-MCMXXV

THE INTERNATIONAL PSYCHO-ANALYTICAL LIBRARY NOS. 7-10.

§ Green cloth printed in gilt.   Dust wrappers not seen. Vol. I: 359 pp. (29), Vol. II: 404 pp. (2), Vol. III: 607 pp. (2), Vol. IV: 508 pp. (2); each $9\frac{3}{4}$ x $6\frac{3}{8}$.

Vols. I & II published November 1924; Vol. III, May 1925; Vol. IV, December 1925. Number of copies printed not known.

NOTE: Volumes II through IV have the imprint "Published by Leonard & Virginia Woolf at The Hogarth Press, 52 Tavistock Square, London, W.C. and The Institute of Psycho-Analysis." All four volumes have "Hogarth Press & The Institute of Psycho-Analysis" on spine (and probably on the dust wrapper).

45. **Fry, Roger** *The Artist and Psycho-Analysis* Published by Leonard and Virginia Woolf at The Hogarth Press, 52 Tavistock Square, London, W.C.1, 1924

THE HOGARTH ESSAYS, FIRST SERIES, NO. 2

§ Cream paper wrappers printed in green.

20 pp. (14) $8\frac{1}{2}$ x $5\frac{1}{2}$.

Published November 1924; number of copies printed not known.

NOTE: Errata slip tipped in opposite title page in some copies.

46. **Graves, Robert** *Mock Beggar Hall* With a cover design by William Nicholson. Published by Leonard & Virginia Woolf at The Hogarth Press 52 Tavistock Square London W.C.1 1924

§ Grey paper boards printed in black.

79 pp. (13) 10 x $7\frac{1}{2}$.

Published May 1924; number of copies not known.

47. **Hobson, Coralie** *In Our Town* Published by Leonard & Virginia Woolf at The Hogarth Press, 52 Tavistock Square, London, W.C. 1924

§ Paper boards decorated in blue, yellow, and purple with orange cloth spine; white label on spine printed in black. White dust wrapper printed in black.
134 pp. (2) $7\frac{1}{2}$ x 5.
Published May 1924; number of copies not known.

48. **Leys, Norman** *Kenya* With an Introduction by Professor Gilbert Murray. Published by Leonard & Virginia Woolf at The Hogarth Press, 52 Tavistock Square, London, W.C. 1924

§ Red cloth printed in gilt. Dust wrapper not seen.
409 pp. (2) $7\frac{7}{8}$ x $5\frac{5}{8}$.
Published November 1924; number of copies not known.
NOTE: Second and third editions were published in 1925 and 1926, each with a new Preface.

49. **Mayor, F. M.** *The Rector's Daughter* Published by Leonard & Virginia Woolf at The Hogarth Press, 52 Tavistock Square, London, W.C. 1924

§ Blue cloth printed in gilt. Dust wrapper not seen.
347 pp. (2) $7\frac{3}{8}$ x 5.
Published May 1924; number of copies not known.

50. **Nicolson, Harold** *Jeanne de Hénaut* Published Privately for the Author by Leonard and Virginia Woolf at The Hogarth Press, 52 Tavistock Square, London, W.C.1 1924

§ Orange paper wrappers; white label printed in black.
23 pp. (3) $7\frac{5}{8}$ x $5\frac{1}{8}$.
Publication date and number of copies not known.
NOTE: I've seen a copy with the printer's "First Proof" stamp and the date "8 Nov. 1924" on the front cover. The author's name is spelled "Nicholson" but this was corrected before publication. •

51. **Ransom, John Crowe** *Grace After Meat* With an Introduction by Robert Graves. Printed & published by Leonard & Virginia Woolf at the Hogarth Press 52 Tavistock Square London W.C. 1924

§ Yellow-gold paper boards printed in white, green, and red; yellow label printed in black.
57 pp. (1) $8\frac{1}{2}$ x $5\frac{1}{2}$.
Published November 1924; 400 copies printed.

52. **Sackville-West, V.** *Seducers in Ecuador* Published by Leonard and Virginia Woolf at The Hogarth Press, 52 Tavistock Square, London, W.C. 1924

§ Marbled red cloth; white label on spine printed in red. Cream dust wrapper printed in red.

74 pp. (2) $6\frac{3}{4}$ x $4\frac{1}{4}$.

Published November 1924; 1,500 copies printed.

53. **Stephen, Leslie** *Some Early Impressions* Published by Leonard & Virginia Woolf at The Hogarth Press, 52 Tavistock Square, London, W.C. 1924

§ Orange cloth printed in gilt. Cream dust wrapper printed in black.

193 pp. (2) 8 x $5\frac{1}{4}$.

Published May 1924; number of copies not known.

54. **Woolf, Virginia** *Mr. Bennett and Mrs. Brown* Published by Leonard and Virginia Woolf at The Hogarth Press Tavistock Square London W.C.1 1924

THE HOGARTH ESSAYS, FIRST SERIES, NO. 1

§ White paper wrappers printed in black.

24 pp. (8) $8\frac{1}{2}$ x $5\frac{1}{2}$.

Published October 1924; 1,000 copies printed.

1925

55. **Aiken, Conrad** *Senlin: A Biography* Published by Leonard and Virginia Woolf at The Hogarth Press Tavistock Square London W.C.1 1925

§ Mauve and pink patterned paper boards; yellow label printed in black.

36 pp. (13) $7\frac{3}{4}$ x $5\frac{1}{4}$.

Published July 1925; number of copies not known.

56. **Békássy, Ferenc** *Adriatica and Other Poems* With a Preface by F. L. Lucas. Published by Leonard & Virginia Woolf at The Hogarth Press 52 Tavistock Square, London, W.C.1 1925

§ Multicolored marbled paper boards; white label printed in black.

58 pp. (3) $7\frac{3}{4}$ x $5\frac{1}{4}$.

Published April 1925; number of copies not known.

57. **Cunard, Nancy** *Parallax* Printed and published by Leonard and Virginia Woolf at The Hogarth Press 52 Tavistock Square London 1925
§ White paper boards printed in black.
24 pp. (1) 9 x $5\frac{5}{8}$.
Published April 1925, about 420 copies printed.

58. **Dobree, Bonamy** *Histriophone A Dialogue on Dramatic Diction* Published by Leonard and Virginia Woolf at The Hogarth Press 52 Tavistock Square London W.C.1 1925
THE HOGARTH ESSAYS, FIRST SERIES, NO. 5
§ Cream paper wrappers printed in black.
40 pp. (13) $8\frac{1}{4}$ x $5\frac{3}{8}$.
Published July 1925; number of copies not known.

59. **Doyle, John** *The Marmosite's Miscellany* Published by Leonard and Virginia Woolf at The Hogarth Press, 52, Tavistock Square, W.C.1 1925
§ Purple, orange, and yellow floral-patterned paper boards; yellow label printed in black.
23 pp. (13) $8\frac{7}{8}$ x $5\frac{7}{8}$.
Published December 1925; number of copies not known.
NOTE: John Doyle is a pseudonym for Robert Graves.

60. **Fay, Mrs. Eliza** *Original Letters from India* (*1779-1815*) With Introductory and Terminal Notes by E. M. Forster. Published by Leonard & Virginia Woolf at the Hogarth Press, 52 Tavistock Square, London, W.C. 1925
§ Green cloth boards printed in gilt. Pale green dust wrapper printed in black.
288 pp. (2) $9\frac{1}{4}$ x $5\frac{1}{2}$.
Published May 1925; 1,500 to 2,000 copies printed; 210 copies pulped in November 1932.

61. **Forster, E. M.** *Anonymity An Enquiry* Published by Leonard & Virginia Woolf at the Hogarth Press, 52 Tavistock Square, London, W.C. 1925
THE HOGARTH ESSAYS, FIRST SERIES, NO. 12
§ Pale green paper boards printed in black (see note).
23 pp. (22) $8\frac{1}{2}$ x $5\frac{1}{2}$.
Published December 1925; 2,000 copies printed.
NOTE: Some copies were bound in pale green paper wrappers.

62. **Gates, Barrington** *Poems* Published by Leonard & Virginia Woolf at The Hogarth Press 52 Tavistock Square, London, W.C.1 1925
§ Red and black marbled paper boards; white label printed in black.
112 pp. (3) $7\frac{1}{4}$ x 5.
Published November 1925; number of copies not known.

63. **Graves, Robert** *Contemporary Techniques of Poetry A Political Analogy* Published by Leonard & Virginia Woolf at The Hogarth Press 52 Tavistock Square. London, W.C.1 1925
THE HOGARTH ESSAYS, FIRST SERIES, NO. 8
§ Pale blue paper boards printed in black.
47 pp. (3) $8\frac{1}{2}$ x $5\frac{1}{2}$.
Published July 1925; number of copies not known.

64. **Harrison, Jane Ellen** *Reminiscences of a Student's Life* Published by Leonard and Virginia Woolf at the Hogarth Press, 52 Tavistock Square, London, W.C. 1925
§ Red and black mottled cloth; white label on spine printed in red. Cream dust wrapper printed in red.
91 pp. (2) $6\frac{3}{4}$ x $4\frac{1}{4}$.
Published November 1925; number of copies not known.

65. **Innes, Kathleen E.** *The Story of The League of Nations Told for Young People* Published by Leonard and Virginia Woolf at The Hogarth Press, 52 Tavistock Square, London. 1925

§ Blue cloth wrappers printed in black.

60 pp. (3) $7\frac{1}{4}$ x $4\frac{7}{8}$.

Published April 1925; number of copies not known.

66. **Keynes, John Maynard** *The Economic Consequences of Mr. Churchill.* Published by Leonard and Virginia Woolf at the Hogarth Press 52, Tavistock Square, W.C.1 1925

§ Green paper wrappers printed in black.

32 pp. (8) $8\frac{3}{8}$ x $5\frac{1}{2}$.

Published July 1925; 7,000 copies printed.

67. **Keynes, John Maynard** *A Short View of Russia* Published by Leonard & Virginia Woolf at The Hogarth Press 52 Tavistock Square, London, W.C.1 1925

THE HOGARTH ESSAYS, FIRST SERIES, NO. 13

§ Pale blue paper boards printed in black.

28 pp. (3) $8\frac{1}{2}$ x $5\frac{1}{2}$.

Published December 1925; number of copies not known.

68. **Kitchin, C. H. B.** *Streamers Waving* Published by Leonard & Virginia Woolf at The Hogarth Press, 52 Tavistock Square, London, W.C. 1925

§ Orange cloth printed in gilt.   Brown dust wrapper printed in dark brown.

172 pp. (2) $7\frac{1}{2}$ x 5.

Published April 1925; number of copies not known.

69. **Lubbock, Alan** *The Character of John Dryden* Published by Leonard & Virginia Woolf at The Hogarth Press 52 Tavistock Square, London, W.C.1 1925

THE HOGARTH ESSAYS, FIRST SERIES, NO. 9

§ White paper wrappers printed in black.

31 pp. (3) $8\frac{1}{2}$ x $5\frac{1}{2}$.

Published July 1925; number of copies not known.

70. **Muir, Edwin** *First Poems* Published by Leonard & Virginia Woolf at The Hogarth Press 52 Tavistock Square, London, W.C.1 1925
§ Multicolored marbled paper boards; white label printed in black.
74 pp. (3) $7\frac{3}{8}$ x 5.
Published April 1925; number of copies not known.

71. **Muir, Willa** *Women: An Inquiry* Published by Leonard & Virginia Woolf at The Hogarth Press 52 Tavistock Square, London, W.C.1 1925
THE HOGARTH ESSAYS, FIRST SERIES, NO. 10
§ White paper wrappers printed in black.
40 pp. (3) $8\frac{1}{2}$ x $5\frac{1}{2}$.
Published October 1925; number of copies not known.

72. **Palmer, Herbert E.** *Songs of Salvation Sin & Satire* Printed & published by Leonard & Virginia Woolf at The Hogarth Press, 52 Tavistock Square, London, W.C.
§ Reddish blue marbled paper boards; white label printed in black.
32 pp. (1) $8\frac{1}{2}$ x $5\frac{1}{2}$.
Published October 1925; about 300 copies printed.
NOTE: The title page is undated, but the Preface is dated 1925. The 1939 Catalogue of The Hogarth Press lists this title 1923.

73. **Plomer, William** *Turbott Wolfe* Published by Leonard & Virginia Woolf at The Hogarth Press, 52 Tavistock Square, W.C.1 1925 (1926)
§ Brown cloth printed in gilt. Buff dust wrapper printed in black.
231 pp. (2) $7\frac{1}{2}$ x 5.
Published March 1926; number of copies not known.

74. **Read, Herbert** *In Retreat* Published by Leonard & Virginia Woolf at The Hogarth Press 52 Tavistock Square, London, W.C.1 1925
THE HOGARTH ESSAYS, FIRST SERIES, NO. 6
§ White paper wrappers printed in black.
43 pp. (3) $8\frac{1}{2}$ x $5\frac{1}{2}$.
Published October 1925; number of copies not known.
NOTE: Folding map in rear.

75. **Rylands, George** *Russet and Taffeta* Printed & published by Leonard & Virginia Woolf at The Hogarth Press, 52 Tavistock Square, London. 1925
§ Brown and black marbled paper wrappers; cream label printed in black.
8 pp. (1) $10\frac{1}{4}$ x 8.
Published December 1925; about 300 copies printed.

76. **Sitwell, Edith** *Poetry & Criticism* Published by Leonard & Virginia Woolf at The Hogarth Press   52 Tavistock Square, London, W.C.1 1925
THE HOGARTH ESSAYS, FIRST SERIES, NO. 11
§ White paper wrappers printed in black (see note).
28 pp. (3) $8\frac{1}{2}$ x $5\frac{1}{2}$.
Published October 1925; number of copies not known.
NOTE: Fifoot's bibliography of the Sitwells calls for pale blue paper wrappers. Both colors were used in this Series and, in this case at least, the printer obviously used whatever stock was convenient.

77. **Thompson, Edward** *The Other Side of the Medal* Published by Leonard & Virginia Woolf at The Hogarth Press 52 Tavistock Square, London, W.C.1 1925
§ Green cloth printed in gilt. Cream dust wrapper printed in black.
143 pp. (3) $7\frac{3}{8}$ x $4\frac{3}{4}$.
Published November 1925; number of copies not known.

78. **Trevelyan R. C.** *Poems and Fables* Printed and published by Leonard and Virginia Woolf at 52 Tavistock Square London W.C. 1925
§ Multicolored marbled paper boards; cream label printed in black.
23 pp. (1) $8\frac{3}{4}$ x $5\frac{1}{2}$.
Published April 1925; about 300 copies printed.
NOTE: "The Hogarth Press" does not appear on the title page.

79. **Woolf, Leonard**   *Fear and Politics A Debate at the Zoo* Published by Leonard and Virginia Woolf at The Hogarth Press, Tavistock Square, London, W.C.1 1925
THE HOGARTH ESSAYS, FIRST SERIES, NO. 7
§ Cream paper wrappers printed in black.
24 pp. (13) $8\frac{1}{2}$ x $5\frac{1}{2}$.
Published July 1925; number of copies not known.

80. **Woolf, Leonard** *Empire and Commerce in Africa A Study in Economic Imperialism.*
> NOTE: I haven't seen a copy of this book but understand that it was one of The Hogarth Press' "Cheap Editions," a reprint, first published in 1920 by George Allen and Unwin for The Labour Research Department.

81. **Woolf, Virginia** *The Common Reader* Published by Leonard & Virginia Woolf at The Hogarth Press, 52 Tavistock Square London, W.C. 1925
> § White paper boards printed in brown and green; grey cloth spine printed in black. Cream dust wrapper printed in brown, green, and black (see note).
> 305 pp. (2) $8\frac{5}{8}$ x $5\frac{5}{8}$.
> Published April 1925; 1,250 copies printed.
> NOTE: There is a secondary binding, grey cloth.

82. **Woolf, Virginia** *Mrs. Dalloway* Published by Leonard & Virginia Woolf at The Hogarth Press, 52 Tavistock Square, London, W.C. 1925
> § Deep rust cloth boards printed in gilt. Cream dust wrapper printed in black and yellow.
> 293 pp. (2) $7\frac{3}{8}$ x 5.
> Published May 1925; about 2,000 copies printed.

1926

83. **Ainslie, Douglas** *Chosen Poems* With a Preface by G.K. Chesterton. Published by Leonard & Virginia Woolf at The Hogarth Press 52 Tavistock Square, London, W.C.1 1926
> § Multicolored marbled paper boards; white label on spine printed in black.
> 168 pp. (3) $6\frac{3}{4}$ x $4\frac{1}{8}$.
> Published March 1926; number of copies not known.
> NOTE: Also issued in a "deluxe edition," bound in quarter brown cloth on grey paper boards printed in gilt and measuring $9\frac{1}{8}$ x $5\frac{7}{8}$.

84. **Arnold-Forster, W,** *The Victory of Reason A Pamphlet on Arbitration* With a letter by Benjamin Franklin. Published by Leonard & Virginia Woolf, at The Hogarth Press, 52 Tavistock Square, London, W.C.1 1926
> § Paper-backed red cloth wrappers printed in black.
> 88 pp. (3) $7\frac{1}{4}$ x $4\frac{7}{8}$.
> Published March 1926; number of copies not known.

85. **Burtt, Joseph** *The People of Ararat* Under the auspices of The Armenian Committee of the Society of Friends. Published by Leonard and Virginia Woolf at The Hogarth Press, 52 Tavistock Square, London 1926
§ Blue cloth printed in gilt. Dust wrapper not seen.
184 pp. (2) $7\frac{3}{4}$ x $4\frac{7}{8}$.
Published November 1926; number of copies not known.
NOTE: Also issued in blue paper wrappers printed in black.
Listed in 1939 Hogarth Catalogue as "Ararat" and dated 1927.

86. **Cameron, Julia Margaret** *Victorian Photographs of Famous Men & Fair Women* With Introductions by Virginia Woolf and Roger Fry. Published by Leonard & Virginia Woolf at The Hogarth Press, London, 1926
§ Pink paper boards; vellum spine printed in gilt. Pale pink dust wrapper similar to covers.
15 pp. plus 24 plates (with tissue guards) (18) $12\frac{3}{4}$ x 10.
Published October 1926; 450 numbered copies printed.

87. **Dobree, Bonamy** *Rochester A Conversation between Sir George Etherege and Mr. Fitzjames* Published by Leonard & Virginia Woolf at The Hogarth Press, 52 Tavistock Square, London, W.C.1 1926
THE HOGARTH ESSAYS, SECOND SERIES, NO. 2
§ Blue-green paper boards printed in black.
50 pp. (3) $6\frac{5}{8}$ x $4\frac{1}{4}$.
Published November 1926; 1,000 copies printed.

88. **Edwards, Mary Stella** *Time and Chance Poems* With a Preface by Professor Gilbert Murray. Published by Leonard & Virginia Woolf at The Hogarth Press, 52 Tavistock Square, London, W.C.1 1926
§ Red, yellow, and grey marbled paper boards; white label printed in black.
63 pp. (3) $7\frac{1}{4}$ x $4\frac{7}{8}$.
Published October 1926; number of copies not known.

89. **Ferenczi, Sandor** *Further Contributions to the Theory and Technique of Psycho-Analysis* Compiled by John Rickman; authorized translation from the German by Jane Isabel Suttie, and others. Published by Leonard & Virginia Woolf at the Hogarth Press, 52 Tavistock Square, London, W.C. and The Institute of Psycho-Analysis MCMXXVI (1927) (Cont'd)

§ Green cloth printed in gilt. Dust wrapper not seen.
473 pp. (2) $9\frac{3}{4} \times 6\frac{3}{8}$.
Published January 1927; number of copies not known.

90. **Fry, Roger** *Art and Commerce* Published by Leonard
& Virginia Woolf at The Hogarth Press 52 Tavistock
Square, London, W.C.1 1926
THE HOGARTH ESSAYS, FIRST SERIES, NO. 16
§ Cream paper wrappers printed in black.
23 pp. (3) $8\frac{5}{8} \times 5\frac{1}{2}$.
Publication date and number of copies printed not known.

91. **Gottschalk, Laura Riding** *The Close Chaplet* Published by
Leonard & Virginia Woolf at The Hogarth Press 52
Tavistock Square, London, W.C.1 1926
§ Blue paper boards; cream paper label printed in black.
77 pp. (3) $7\frac{1}{2} \times 5$.
Published October 1926; number of copies not known.

92. **Graves, Robert** *Another Future of Poetry* Published by
Leonard & Virginia Woolf at The Hogarth Press 52
Tavistock Square, London, W.C.1 1926
THE HOGARTH ESSAYS, FIRST SERIES, NO. 18
§ Pale blue paper boards printed in black.
33 pp. (3) $8\frac{1}{2} \times 5\frac{1}{2}$.
Published July 1926; 1,000 copies printed.

93. **Graves, Robert** *Impenetrability or The Proper Habit of English*
Published by Leonard & Virginia Woolf at The Hogarth
Press, 52 Tavistock Square, London, W.C.1 1926 (1927)
THE HOGARTH ESSAYS, SECOND SERIES, NO. 3
§ Blue-green paper boards printed in black.
62 pp. (3) $6\frac{5}{8} \times 4\frac{1}{4}$.
Published March 1927; number of copies not known.

94. **Hobson, J. A.** *Notes on Law and Order.* Published by
Leonard & Virginia Woolf at The Hogarth Press 52
Tavistock Square London, W.C.1 1926
THE HOGARTH ESSAYS, FIRST SERIES, NO. 14
§ Pale blue paper wrappers printed in black.
31 pp. (3) $8\frac{1}{2} \times 5\frac{1}{2}$.
Published March 1926; number of copies not known.

95. **Innes, Kathleen E.** *How The League of Nations Works Told for Young People* Published by Leonard and Virginia Woolf at The Hogarth Press, 52 Tavistock Square, London 1926
§ Paper-backed blue cloth wrappers printed in black.
64 pp. (3) $7\frac{1}{4}$ x $4\frac{7}{8}$.
Published March 1926; 2,500 copies printed.

96. **Jaeger, M.** *The Question Mark* Published by Leonard & Virginia Woolf at The Hogarth Press 52 Tavistock Square, London, W.C.1 1926
§ Red cloth printed in blue. Cream dust wrapper printed in black.
252 pp. (3) $7\frac{3}{8}$ x $4\frac{7}{8}$.
Published March 1926; number of copies not known.

97. **Keynes, John Maynard** *The End of Laissez-Faire* Published by Leonard & Virginia Woolf at The Hogarth Press, 52 Tavistock Square, London, W.C.1 1926
§ Blue paper boards; grey cloth spine; white label on spine printed in blue. Cream dust wrapper printed in blue.
54 pp. (3) $7\frac{3}{8}$ x $4\frac{7}{8}$.
Published July 1926; 2,000 copies printed.

98. **Lee, Vernon** *The Poet's Eye* Published by Leonard & Virginia Woolf at The Hogarth Press 52 Tavistock Square, London, W.C.1 1926
THE HOGARTH ESSAYS, FIRST SERIES, NO. 17
§ White paper wrappers printed in black.
19 pp. (3) $8\frac{1}{2}$ x $5\frac{1}{2}$.
Published July 1926; 1,000 copies printed.
NOTE: Vernon Lee was the pseudonym of Violet Paget.

99. **Lucas, F. L.** *The River Flows* Published by Leonard & Virginia Woolf at The Hogarth Press, 52 Tavistock Square, London, W.C. 1926
§ Green cloth printed in gilt. Dust wrapper not seen.
204 pp. (2) $7\frac{1}{2}$ x 5.
Published October 1926; number of copies not known.

100. **Lyle, Marius** *The Education of a Young Man in Twelve Lessons* Published by Leonard & Virginia Woolf at The Hogarth Press, 52 Tavistock Square, London, W.C. 1926
§ Green cloth printed in gilt. White dust wrapper printed in black.
299 pp. (2) $7\frac{1}{2}$ x 5.
Published March 1926; number of copies not known.

101. **Macaulay, Rose** *Catchwords and Claptrap* Published by Leonard & Virginia Woolf at The Hogarth Press, 52 Tavistock Square, London, W.C.1 1926
THE HOGARTH ESSAYS, SECOND SERIES, NO. 4
§ Blue-green paper boards printed in black.
45 pp. (3) $6\frac{5}{8}$ x $4\frac{1}{4}$.
Published November 1926; number of copies not known.

102. **Manning-Sanders, Ruth** *Martha Wish-You-Ill* Printed & published by Leonard & Virginia Woolf at The Hogarth Press, London. 1926
§ Multicolored marbled paper wrappers; cream label printed in black.
16 pp. (1) $8\frac{3}{8}$ x $5\frac{1}{2}$.
Published July 1926; about 280 copies printed.
NOTE: Listed under the title "Martin Wish-You-Ill" in The English Catalogue of Books.

103. **Martin, Kingsley** *The British Public and The General Strike* Published by Leonard & Virginia Woolf at The Hogarth Press, 52 Tavistock Square, London, W.C.1 1926
§ Blue paper boards; grey cloth spine; white label on spine printed in black. Buff dust wrapper printed in black.
128 pp. (3) $7\frac{1}{2}$ x $4\frac{7}{8}$.
Published November 1926; number of copies not known.

104. **Muir, Edwin** *Chorus of the Newly Dead* Printed & published by Leonard & Virginia Woolf at The Hogarth Press, London. 1926
§ Multicolored marbled paper wrappers; yellow label printed in black.
16 pp. (1) $8\frac{3}{8}$ x $5\frac{3}{8}$.
Published July 1926; about 315 copies printed.

105. **Muir, Edwin** *Transition   Essays on Contemporary Literature*
1926 Published by Leonard and Virginia Woolf at The
Hogarth Press, 52 Tavistock Square, London
§ Red cloth; white label on spine printed in black. Issued
without dust wrapper.
218 pp. (6) $7\frac{3}{4}$ x $5\frac{1}{4}$.
Published October 1926; number of copies not known.

106. **Noel Baker, Professor P. J.** *Disarmament* The Hogarth
Press 52, Tavistock Square, W.C.3 1926
§ Red cloth printed in gilt. Cream dust wrapper printed
in brown.
352 pp. (19) $8\frac{3}{4}$ x $5\frac{1}{2}$.
Published April 1926; number of copies not known.

107. **Sackville-West, V.** *Passenger to Teheran* Published by
Leonard and Virginia Woolf at the Hogarth Press, 52
Tavistock Square, London, W.C. 1926
§ Brown marbled cloth printed in gilt. White dust wrap-
per printed in black.
181 pp. (2) $8\frac{3}{4}$ x $5\frac{3}{4}$.
Published November 1926; 1,640 copies printed.

108. **S(anger), C. P.** *The Structure of Wuthering Heights by C.P.S.*
Published by Leonard & Virginia Woolf at The Hogarth
Press 52 Tavistock Square, London, W.C.1 1926
THE HOGARTH ESSAYS, FIRST SERIES, NO. 19
§ White paper wrappers printed in black.
24 pp. (3) $8\frac{1}{2}$ x $5\frac{1}{2}$.
Published July 1926; number of copies not known.
NOTE: Sometimes wrongly attributed to C. P. Snow.

109. **Snaith, Stanley** *April Morning* Printed & published by
Leonard & Virginia Woolf at The Hogarth Press, London 1926
§ Multicolored marbled paper wrappers; white label
printed in black.
24 pp. (1) $8\frac{1}{4}$ x $5\frac{1}{2}$.
Published October 1926; about 260 copies printed.

110. **Stein, Gertrude** *Composition as Explanation* Published by Leonard & Virginia Woolf at The Hogarth Press, 52 Tavistock Square, London, W.C.1 1926
THE HOGARTH ESSAYS, SECOND SERIES, NO. 1
§ Blue-green paper boards printed in black.
59 pp. (3) $6\frac{5}{8}$ x $4\frac{1}{4}$.
Published November 1926; number of copies not known.

111. **Tree, Viola** *Castles in the Air The Story of my Singing Days* Published by Leonard & Virginia Woolf at the Hogarth Press, 52 Tavistock Square, London, W.C.1 1926
§ Grey-green cloth printed in gilt. Dust wrapper not seen.
326 pp. (3) 9 x $5\frac{1}{2}$.
Published April 1926; number of copies not known.

112. **Trevelyan, R. C.** *The Deluge and Other Poems* Published by Leonard & Virginia Woolf at The Hogarth Press 52 Tavistock Square, London, W.C.1 1926
§ Yellow, black, and red marbled paper boards; white label printed in black.
47 pp. (3) $8\frac{5}{8}$ x $5\frac{1}{2}$.
Published March 1926; 400 copies printed.

113. **Waley, Hubert** *The Revival of Aesthetics* Published by Leonard & Virginia Woolf at The Hogarth Press 52 Tavistock Square, London, W.C.1 1926
THE HOGARTH ESSAYS, FIRST SERIES, NO. 15
§ Pale blue paper wrappers printed in black.
40 pp. (3) $8\frac{1}{2}$ x $5\frac{1}{2}$.
Published March 1926; number of copies not known.

1 9 2 7

114. **Abraham, Karl** *Selected Papers of Karl Abraham* With an Introductory Memoir by Ernest Jones. Translated by Douglas Bryan and Alix Strachey. Published by Leonard & Virginia Woolf at The Hogarth Press, 52 Tavistock Square, London, W.C. and The Institute of Psycho-Analysis. 1927
THE INTERNATIONAL PSYCHO-ANALYTICAL LIBRARY NO. 13
§ Green cloth printed in gilt. Dust wrapper not seen.
527 pp. (2) $9\frac{1}{4}$ x $5\frac{3}{4}$.
Published September 1927; 750 copies printed.

115. **Alexander, Horace G.** *Justice Among Nations* Published by Leonard & Virginia Woolf at The Hogarth Press, 52 Tavistock Square, London, W.C.1 1927

FIRST MERTTENS LECTURE ON WAR AND PEACE

§ Blue paper boards, grey cloth spine with white label printed in black. Cream dust wrapper printed in black (see note).

59 pp. (3) $7\frac{1}{2}$ x 5.

Published February 1927; 1,500 copies printed.

NOTE: Also issued in green paper wrappers printed in black measuring $7\frac{1}{4}$ x $4\frac{7}{8}$.

116. **Braithwaite, R. B.** *The State of Religious Belief An Inquiry Based on "The Nation and Athenaeum" Questionnaire* Published by Leonard & Virginia Woolf at The Hogarth Press, 52 Tavistock Square, London, W.C.1 1927

§ Green cloth; white label on spine printed in black. Cream dust wrapper printed in black.

77 pp. (3) $7\frac{1}{2}$ x 5.

Published February 1927; number of copies not known.

117. **Davies, Charles** *Welshman's Way* Published by Leonard & Virginia Woolf at The Hogarth Press, 52 Tavistock Square, London, W.C.1 1927

HOGARTH STORIES, NO. 2

§ Cream paper wrappers printed in brown and green.

127 pp. (3) $6\frac{3}{4}$ x $4\frac{1}{2}$.

Published October 1927; number of copies not known.

118. **Demant, V. A., Philippe Mairet, Albert Newsome, Alan Porter, Maurice B. Reckitt, Egerton Swann, W. T. Symons** *Coal A Challenge to the National Conscience* Published by Leonard & Virginia Woolf at The Hogarth Press, 52 Tavistock Square, London, W.C.1 1927

§ Green cloth; white label on spine printed in black. Yellow dust wrapper printed in black.

84 pp. (3) $7\frac{3}{8}$ x $4\frac{7}{8}$.

Published April 1927; number of copies not known.

NOTE: "Edited by Alan Porter" on spine.

119. **Freud, Sigmund** *The Ego and the Id* Authorized Translation by Joan Riviere. Published by Leonard & Virginia Woolf at The Hogarth Press, 52 Tavistock Square, London, W.C and the Institute of Psycho-Analysis. 1927
THE INTERNATIONAL PSYCHO-ANALYTICAL LIBRARY NO. 12
§ Green cloth printed in gilt. Grey dust wrapper printed in black.
88 pp. (2) $9\frac{3}{4}$ x $6\frac{3}{8}$.
Published January 1927; 1,500 copies printed.

120. **Fry, Roger** *Cézanne A Study of his Development* Published by Leonard & Virginia Woolf at The Hogarth Press, London, 1927
§ White paper boards printed in blue; white cloth spine printed in blue. Dust wrapper not seen.
83 pp. plus 40 plates (18) 10 x $7\frac{3}{8}$.
Published November 1927; number of copies not known.

121. **Hull, Robert H.** *Contemporary Music* Published by Leonard and Virginia Woolf at The Hogarth Press, 52 Tavistock Square, London, W.C.1 1927
THE HOGARTH ESSAYS, SECOND SERIES, NO. 10
§ Grey paper wrappers printed in red.
45 pp. (3) $6\frac{5}{8}$ x $4\frac{1}{8}$.
Published October 1927; number of copies not known.

122. **Hutchinson, Mary** *Fugitive Pieces* Published by Leonard and Virginia Woolf at The Hogarth Press, 52 Tavistock Square, London, W.C. 1927
§ Red cloth printed in gilt. Pale blue dust wrapper printed in black.
210 pp. (2) $7\frac{3}{8}$ x $4\frac{3}{4}$.
Published June 1927; 1,000 copies printed.
NOTE: "(To be continued.)" appears on last page of text but nothing further was published by The Hogarth Press.

123. **Ibbetson, Peter** *Mr. Baldwin Explains and other Dream Interviews* Published by Leonard & Virginia Woolf at The Hogarth Press, 52 Tavistock Square, London, W.C.1 1927

§ Green cloth; white label on spine printed in black. White dust wrapper printed in black.

143 pp. (3) $7\frac{3}{8}$ x $4\frac{3}{4}$.

Published October 1927; number of copies not known.

124. **Innes, Kathleen E.** *The League of Nations and the World's Workers An Introduction to the Work of the International Labour Organisation* Published by Leonard and Virginia Woolf at The Hogarth Press, 52 Tavistock Square, London 1927

§ Light green paper wrappers printed in black.

48 pp. (3) $7\frac{1}{8}$ x $4\frac{3}{4}$.

Published April 1927; 2,500 copies printed.

125. **Jaeger, M.** *The Man with Six Senses* Published by Leonard & Virginia Woolf at The Hogarth Press, 52 Tavistock Square, London, W.C.1 1927

§ Yellow-orange cloth printed in gilt. Dust wrapper not seen.

272 pp. (8) $7\frac{1}{2}$ x 5.

Published September 1927; number of copies not known.

126. **King-Hall, Stephen** *The China of To-Day* Published by Leonard & Virginia Woolf at The Hogarth Press, 52 Tavistock Square, London, W.C.1 1927

§ Blue paper boards; grey cloth spine; white label on spine printed in black. Cream dust wrapper printed in black.

45 pp. (3) $7\frac{1}{2}$ x 5.

Published February 1927; 1,500 copies printed.

127. **King-Hall, Stephen** *Posterity* Published by Leonard & Virginia Woolf at The Hogarth Press, 52 Tavistock Square, London, W.C.1 1927

THE HOGARTH ESSAYS, SECOND SERIES, NO. 9

§ Grey paper wrappers printed in red.

45 pp. (3) $6\frac{5}{8}$ x $4\frac{1}{8}$.

Published October 1927; 1,000 copies printed.

128. **Kitchin, C. H. B.** *Mr. Balcony* Published by Leonard & Virginia Woolf at The Hogarth Press, 52 Tavistock Square, London, W.C. 1927
§ Blue cloth printed in gilt. Pale blue dust wrapper printed in black and ochre.
223 pp. (2) $7\frac{1}{2}$ x 5.
Published October 1927; 1,000 copies printed.

129. **Lucas, F. L.** *Tragedy in relation to Aristotle's* POETICS Published by Leonard & Virginia Woolf at The Hogarth Press, 52 Tavistock Square, London, W.C.1 1927 (1928)
HOGARTH LECTURES ON LITERATURE, FIRST SERIES, NO. 2
§ Orange cloth printed in red. Orange dust wrapper printed in red.
158 pp. (3) $7\frac{1}{2}$ x $4\frac{7}{8}$.
Published February 1928; 2,020 copies printed.
NOTE: Attributed to E. V. Lucas in The English Catalogue of Books.

130. **Mann, F. O.** *The Sisters and Other Tales in Verse* Published by Leonard & Virginia Woolf at The Hogarth Press, 52 Tavistock Square, London, W.C.1 1927
§ Orange paper wrappers; white label printed in black.
99 pp. (3) $7\frac{5}{8}$ x 5.
Published September 1927; number of copies not known.

131. **Mauron, Charles** *The Nature of Beauty in Art and Literature* Translation and Preface by Roger Fry. Published by Leonard & Virginia Woolf at The Hogarth Press, 52 Tavistock Square, London, W.C.1 1927
THE HOGARTH ESSAYS, SECOND SERIES, NO. 6
§ Blue-green paper boards printed in black.
88 pp. (3) $6\frac{5}{8}$ x $4\frac{1}{4}$.
Published March 1927; 1,000 copies printed.

132. **Muir, Edwin** *The Marionette* Published by Leonard & Virginia Woolf at The Hogarth Press, 52 Tavistock Square, London, W.C.1 1927
§ Greyish brown cloth printed in gilt. Pale green dust wrapper printed in red.
155 pp. (8) $7\frac{1}{2}$ x 5.
Published May 1927; number of copies not known.

133. Nansen, Fridtjof *Adventure and Other Papers* Published by Leonard & Virginia Woolf at The Hogarth Press, 52 Tavistock Square, London, W.C.1 1927

§ Green cloth; white label on spine printed in black. Cream dust wrapper printed in black.

82 pp. (3) $7\frac{3}{8}$ x $4\frac{7}{8}$.

Published May 1927; 1,000 copies printed.

134. Nation, The *Books and the Public* By the Editor of THE NATION, John Maynard Keynes, Stanley Unwin, Michael Sadlier, Basil Blackwell, Leonard Woolf, Peter Ibbetson, Henry B. Saxton, Charles Young, Jeffery E. Jeffery. Published by Leonard & Virginia Woolf at The Hogarth Press, 52 Tavistock Square, London, W.C.1 1927

§ Green paper wrappers printed in black.

70 pp. (3) $7\frac{1}{4}$ x $4\frac{7}{8}$.

Published September 1927; number of copies not known.

135. Nicoll, Allardyce *Studies in Shakespeare* Published by Leonard & Virginia Woolf at The Hogarth Press, 52 Tavistock Square, London, W.C.1 1927 (1928)

HOGARTH LECTURES ON LITERATURE, FIRST SERIES, NO. 3

§ Orange cloth printed in red. Orange dust wrapper printed in red.

164 pp. (3) $7\frac{1}{2}$ x $4\frac{7}{8}$.

Published February 1928; number of copies not known.

136. Nicolson, Harold *The Development of English Biography* Published by Leonard & Virginia Woolf at The Hogarth Press, 52 Tavistock Square, London, W.C.1 1927 (1928)

HOGARTH LECTURES ON LITERATURE, FIRST SERIES, NO. 4

§ Orange cloth printed in red. Orange dust wrapper printed in red.

158 pp. (3) $7\frac{1}{2}$ x $4\frac{7}{8}$.

Published February 1928; 2,020 copies printed.

137. Noel Baker, Professor P. J. *Disarmament and the Coolidge Conference* Published by Leonard & Virginia Woolf at The Hogarth Press, 52 Tavistock Square, London, W.C.1 1927

§ Brown paper wrappers printed in black.

53 pp. (5) $6\frac{7}{8}$ x $4\frac{1}{2}$.

Published November 1927; 1,000 copies printed.

138. **Olivier, Lord** *The Anatomy of African Misery* Published by Leonard & Virginia Woolf at The Hogarth Press, 52 Tavistock Square, London, W.C.1 1927
§ Black cloth; white label on spine printed in black. Cream dust wrapper printed in black.
234 pp. (3) $7\frac{5}{8}$ x 5.
Published March 1927; 1,500 copies printed.

139. **Olivier, Lord** *The Empire Builder* Published by Leonard & Virginia Woolf at The Hogarth Press, 52 Tavistock Square, London, W.C.1 1927
HOGARTH STORIES, NO. 1
§ White paper boards printed in brown and green.
48 pp. (3) $6\frac{3}{4}$ x $4\frac{1}{4}$.
Published May 1927; number of copies not known.

140. **Palmer, Herbert Edward** *The Judgment of Francois Villon A Pageant-Episode Play in Five Acts* Published by Leonard and Virginia Woolf at The Hogarth Press, 52 Tavistock Square, London, W.C. 1927
§ Red and black marbled cloth; imitation vellum spine printed in gilt. Purple dust wrapper printed in black.
138 pp. (2) $9\frac{1}{8}$ x 6.
Published November 1927; limited to 400 numbered and signed copies.

141. **Phibbs, Geoffrey** *Withering of the Fig Leaf* Published by Leonard & Virginia Woolf at The Hogarth Press, 52 Tavistock Square, London, W.C.1 1927
§ Orange paper wrappers; white label printed in black.
45 pp. (3) $7\frac{1}{2}$ x $4\frac{7}{8}$.
Publication date and number of copies printed not known.

142. **Plomer, William** *I Speak of Africa* Published by Leonard & Virginia Woolf at The Hogarth Press, 52 Tavistock Square, London, W.C. 1927
§ Red cloth printed in gilt. Black dust wrapper printed in white.
258 pp. (2) $7\frac{1}{2}$ x 5.
Published September 1927; number of copies not known.

143. **Plomer, William** *Notes for Poems* Published by Leonard & Virginia Woolf at The Hogarth Press, 52 Tavistock Square, London, W.C.1 1927 (1928)
§ Yellow cloth printed in gilt. Plain tissue dust wrapper.
98 pp. (5) $7\frac{1}{2}$ x 5.
Published March 1928; 450 copies printed.

144. **Quiller-Couch, Sir Arthur** *A Lecture on Lectures* Introductory Volume. Published by Leonard & Virginia Woolf at The Hogarth Press, 52 Tavistock Square, London, W.C.1 1927 (1928)
HOGARTH LECTURES ON LITERATURE, FIRST SERIES, NO. 1
§ Orange cloth printed in red. Orange dust wrapper printed in red (see note).
48 pp. (3) $7\frac{1}{2}$ x $4\frac{7}{8}$.
Published February 1928; 2,020 copies printed.
NOTE: There is a variant binding using a cloth with a rougher texture, and without the decorative border.

145. **Riding, Laura** *Voltaire A Biographical Fantasy* Printed & published by L. & V. Woolf at The Hogarth Press, 52 Tavistock Square 1927
§ Black paper wrappers; cream label printed in black.
30 pp. (1) $8\frac{1}{8}$ x $5\frac{3}{8}$.
Published November 1927; about 250 copies printed.

NOTE: The author's name was printed on the title page as Laura Riding Gottschalk, but Gottschalk was over-printed with two lines.

146. **Sackville West, Edward** *The Apology of Arthur Rimbaud A Dialogue* Published by Leonard & Virginia Woolf at The Hogarth Press, 52 Tavistock Square, London, W.C.1 1927

THE HOGARTH ESSAYS, SECOND SERIES, NO. 7

§ Blue-green paper boards printed in black.

74 pp. (3) $6\frac{5}{8}$ x $4\frac{1}{4}$.

Published March 1927; 1,000 copies printed.

147. **Sanders, Wm. Stephen** *Early Socialist Days* Published by Leonard & Virginia Woolf at The Hogarth Press, 52 Tavistock Square, London, W.C.1 1927

§ Yellow paper boards; grey cloth spine; red labels printed in black on top cover and spine. Yellow dust wrapper printed in black.

101 pp. (3) $7\frac{1}{2}$ x 5.

Published September 1927; number of copies not known.

148. **Smith, Logan Pearsall** *The Prospects of Literature* Published by Leonard & Virginia Woolf at The Hogarth Press, 52 Tavistock Square, London, W.C.1 1927

THE HOGARTH ESSAYS, SECOND SERIES, NO. 8

§ Grey paper wrappers printed in red.

35 pp. (3) $6\frac{5}{8}$ x $4\frac{1}{8}$.

Published October 1927; number of copies not known.

NOTE: With this title the binding style of the Series changed.

149. **Trevelyan, R. C.** *Meleager* Published by Leonard & Virginia Woolf at The Hogarth Press, 52 Tavistock Square, London, W.C.1 1927

§ Multicolored marbled paper boards; white label printed in black.

51 pp. (3) $7\frac{3}{8}$ x 5.

Published March 1927; number of copies (see note).

NOTE: Records surviving at The Hogarth Press state that 300 copies were printed in October 1925. The reason for the delay in publication is not known.

150. **Trevelyan, R. C.** *Cheiron* Published by Leonard & Virginia Woolf at The Hogarth Press, 52 Tavistock Square, London, W.C.1 1927 (1928)

§ Multicolored marbled paper boards; white label printed in black.

58 pp. (5) $7\frac{3}{8}$ x 5.

Published March 1928; 300 copies printed.

151. **Wells, H. G.** *Democracy Under Revision* A Lecture Delivered at the Sorbonne on March 15th, 1927. Published by Leonard & Virginia Woolf at The Hogarth Press, 52 Tavistock Square, London, W.C.1 1927
§ Blue paper boards; grey cloth spine; white label on spine printed in blue. Cream dust wrapper printed in black.
47 pp. (8) $7\frac{1}{2}$ x 5.
Published March 1927; 3,200 copies printed.

152. **Woolf, Leonard** *Hunting the Highbrow* Published by Leonard & Virginia Woolf at The Hogarth Press, 52 Tavistock Square, London, W.C.1 1927
THE HOGARTH ESSAYS, SECOND SERIES, NO. 5
§ Blue-green paper boards printed in black.
52 pp. (3) $6\frac{5}{8}$ x $4\frac{1}{4}$.
Published March 1927; 1,000 copies printed.

153. **Woolf, Leonard** *Essays on Literature, History, Politics, etc.* Published by Leonard and Virginia Woolf at The Hogarth Press, 52 Tavistock Square, London, W.C. 1927
§ Brown cloth printed in gilt. White dust wrapper printed in black.
256 pp. (2) $7\frac{1}{2}$ x 5.
Published May 1927; 1,000 copies printed.

154. **Woolf, Virginia** *To the Lighthouse* Published by Leonard & Virginia Woolf at The Hogarth Press, 52 Tavistock Square, London, W.C. 1927
§ Bright blue cloth printed in gilt. Cream dust wrapper printed in pale blue and black.
320 pp. (2) $7\frac{3}{8}$ x $4\frac{7}{8}$.
Published May 1927; 3,000 copies printed.

155. **Woolf, Virginia** *Kew Gardens* Decorated by Vanessa Bell. Published by The Hogarth Press
§ White paper boards printed in blue, green, and brown. Cellophane dust wrapper.
45 pp. (18) $10\frac{1}{8}$ x $7\frac{1}{2}$. (Text printed on rectos only.)
Published November 1927; 500 numbered copies printed.
NOTE: Third (limited) edition. First published in 1919 (see no. 7). Some copies were signed by author and illustrator.

156. **Bell, Clive** *Proust* Published by Leonard and Virginia
Woolf at The Hogarth Press, 52 Tavistock Square, London, W.C. 1928
§ Red and black mottled cloth; cream label on spine
printed in red. Cream dust wrapper printed in red.
89 pp. (2) $6\frac{3}{4}$ x $4\frac{1}{4}$.
Published November 1928; number of copies not known.

157. **Bowker, B.** *Lancashire Under the Hammer* Published by
Leonard & Virginia Woolf at The Hogarth Press, 52
Tavistock Square, London, W.C.1 1928
§ Green cloth; white label on spine printed in black.
Cream dust wrapper printed in black.
127 pp. (3) $7\frac{3}{8}$ x $4\frac{3}{4}$.
Published March 1928; number of copies not known.

158. **Brookes, Edgar H.** *What is Wrong with the League of Na-
tions? A constructive Criticism of the League of Nations in working,
with certain practical suggestions.* Published by Leonard &
Virginia Woolf at The Hogarth Press, 52 Tavistock
Square, London, W.C.1 1928
§ Buff paper wrappers printed in blue.
38 pp. (5) $7\frac{1}{4}$ x $4\frac{7}{8}$.
Published March 1928; number of copies not known.

159. **Cornford, Frances** *Different Days* Published by Leonard
& Virginia Woolf at The Hogarth Press, 52 Tavistock
Square, London, W.C.1 1928
HOGARTH LIVING POETS, FIRST SERIES, NO. 1
§ Blue-grey paper boards printed in black.
48 pp. (3) $7\frac{1}{2}$ x 5.
Published May 1928; 500 copies printed.

160. **Enfield, D. E.** *L.E.L. A Mystery of the Thirties* Published
by Leonard and Virginia Woolf at The Hogarth Press,
52 Tavistock Square, London 1928
§ Pink, silk-textured cloth printed in black. Pink dust
wrapper printed in black, with a reproduction of the
frontispiece on the front cover.
201 pp. (2) $8\frac{7}{8}$ x $5\frac{3}{4}$.
Published March 1928; number of copies not known.
NOTE: There is a variant binding in rough-textured salmon cloth.

161. **Fitzurse, R.** *It Was Not Jones* Published by Leonard & Virginia Woolf at The Hogarth Press, 52 Tavistock Square, London, W.C.1 1928

HOGARTH LIVING POETS, FIRST SERIES, NO. 2

§ Blue-grey paper boards printed in black.

48 pp. (3) $7\frac{1}{2}$ x 5.

Published May 1928; 500 copies printed.

NOTE: R. Fitzurse is a pseudonym for Geoffrey Phibbs.

162. **Fox, R. M.** *The Triumphant Machine* (*A Study of Machine Civilisation*) Published by Leonard & Virginia Woolf at The Hogarth Press, 52 Tavistock Square, London, W.C.1 1928

§ Olive green cloth; white label on spine printed in black. White dust wrapper printed in black and orange.

148 pp. (5) $7\frac{1}{2}$ x $4\frac{7}{8}$.

Published March 1928; **1,000 copies printed.**

163. **Freud, Sigmund** *The Future of an Illusion* Translated by W. D. Robson-Scott. Published by Leonard & Virginia Woolf at The Hogarth Press, 52 Tavistock Square, London, W.C.1 and The Institute of Psycho-Analysis MCMXXVIII

THE INTERNATIONAL PSYCHO-ANALYTICAL LIBRARY NO. 15

§ Green cloth printed in gilt. Grey dust wrapper printed in black.

98 pp. (2) $9\frac{3}{4}$ x $6\frac{3}{8}$.

Published July 1928; **1,516 copies printed.**

164. **Grierson, H. J. C.** *Lyrical Poetry From Blake to Hardy* Published by Leonard & Virginia Woolf at The Hogarth Press, 52 Tavistock Square, London, W.C.1 1928

HOGARTH LECTURES ON LITERATURE, FIRST SERIES, NO. 5

§ Orange cloth printed in red. Orange dust wrapper printed in red.

159 pp. (3) $7\frac{1}{2}$ x $4\frac{7}{8}$.

Published November 1928; 2,275 copies printed.

NOTE: Announced as in preparation in F.L. Lucas's *Tragedy* (no. 129) under the title *Development of the Nineteenth-Century Lyric.*

165. **Harris, H. Wilson** *Arms or Arbitration?* Published by Leonard & Virginia Woolf, at The Hogarth Press, 52 Tavistock Square, London, W.C.1 1928
§ Chocolate brown cloth wrappers printed in black.
93 pp. (3) $7\frac{3}{8}$ x $4\frac{3}{8}$.
Published March 1928; 1,780 copies printed.

166. **Hull, Robert H.** *Delius* Published by Leonard & Virginia Woolf at The Hogarth Press, 52 Tavistock Square, London, W.C.1 1928
THE HOGARTH ESSAYS, SECOND SERIES, NO. 12
§ Grey paper wrappers printed in red.
45 pp. (3) $6\frac{5}{8}$ x $4\frac{1}{8}$.
Published March 1928; number of copies not known.

167. **Jeffers, Robinson** *Roan Stallion Tamar and Other Poems* Published by Leonard & Virginia Woolf at The Hogarth Press 52, Tavistock Square, London, W.C.1 1928
HOGARTH LIVING POETS, FIRST SERIES, NO. 4
§ Blue-grey paper boards printed in black.
254 pp. (6) 8 x $5\frac{1}{2}$.
Published October 1928; 440 copies issued.

168. **Muir, Edwin** *The Structure of the Novel* Published by Leonard & Virginia Woolf at The Hogarth Press, 52 Tavistock Square, London, W.C.1 1928
HOGARTH LECTURES ON LITERATURE, FIRST SERIES, NO. 6
§ Orange cloth printed in red. Orange dust wrapper printed in red.
151 pp. (3) $7\frac{1}{2}$ x $4\frac{7}{8}$.
Published November 1928; 2,250 copies printed.
NOTE: Announced as in preparation in F.L. Lucas's *Tragedy* (no. 129) under the title *Plot in the Novel.*

169. **Pollard, Francis E.** *War and Human Values* Published by Leonard & Virginia Woolf at The Hogarth Press, 52 Tavistock Square, London, W.C.1 1928
SECOND MERTTENS LECTURE ON WAR AND PEACE
§ Blue paper wrappers printed in black.
72 pp. (3) $7\frac{1}{4}$ x $4\frac{5}{8}$.
Published June 1928; number of copies not known.
NOTE: Also bound in blue cloth printed in black.

170. **Read, Herbert** *Phases of English Poetry* Published by Leonard & Virginia Woolf at The Hogarth Press, 52 Tavistock Square, London, W.C.1 1928

HOGARTH LECTURES ON LITERATURE, FIRST SERIES, NO. 7
§ Orange cloth printed in red. Orange dust wrapper printed in red.
158 pp. (3) $7\frac{1}{2}$ x $4\frac{7}{8}$.
Published November 1928; number of copies not known.

171. **Rhondda, Viscountess** *Leisured Women* Published by Leonard and Virginia Woolf at The Hogarth Press, 52 Tavistock Square, London, W.C.1 1928

THE HOGARTH ESSAYS, SECOND SERIES, NO. 11
§ Grey paper wrappers printed in red.
61 pp. (3) $6\frac{5}{8}$ x $4\frac{1}{8}$.
Published March 1928; 1,000 copies printed.

172. **Rickman, John** *Index Psychoanalyticus 1893-1926 Being an Authors' Index of Papers on Psycho-Analysis* Published by Leonard & Virginia Woolf at The Hogarth Press, 52 Tavistock Square, London, W.C.1 and The Institute of Psycho-Analysis MCMXXVIII

THE INTERNATIONAL PSYCHO-ANALYTICAL LIBRARY NO. 14
§ Green cloth printed in gilt. Dust wrapper not seen.
276 pp. (2) $9\frac{1}{8}$ x $5\frac{3}{4}$.
Month of publication not known; 750 copies printed.

173. **Ritchie, Alice** *The Peacemakers* Published by Leonard & Virginia Woolf at the Hogarth Press, 52 Tavistock Square, London, W.C.1 1928

§ Orange cloth printed in gilt. Grey dust wrapper printed in black.
253 pp. (8) $7\frac{1}{2}$ x $4\frac{7}{8}$.
Published May 1928; 1,000 copies printed.

174. **Robins, Elizabeth** *Ibsen and the Actress* Published by Leonard & Virginia Woolf at The Hogarth Press, 52 Tavistock Square, London, W.C.1 1928

THE HOGARTH ESSAYS, SECOND SERIES, NO. 15
§ Buff paper wrappers printed in brown.
56 pp. (3) $6\frac{5}{8}$ x $4\frac{1}{8}$.
Published October 1928; 1,000 copies printed.

175. **Rylands, George W. H.** *Words and Poetry* With an Introduction by Lytton Strachey. Published by Leonard & Virginia Woolf at The Hogarth Press, 52 Tavistock Square, London, W.C. 1928
§ Yellow cloth printed in gilt. Dust wrapper not seen.
244 pp. (2) $8\frac{5}{8}$ x $5\frac{1}{2}$.
Published May 1928; number of copies not known.

176. **Sackville-West, V.** *Twelve Days An account of a journey across the Bakhtiari Mountains in South-western Persia* Published by Leonard and Virginia Woolf at the Hogarth Press, 52 Tavistock Square, London, W.C. 1928
§ Black and brown marbled cloth printed in gilt. White pictorial dust wrapper printed in black.
143 pp. (2) $8\frac{3}{4}$ x $5\frac{1}{2}$.
Published October 1928; 2,025 copies printed.

177. **Selincourt, Basil De** *The Enjoyment of Music* Published by Leonard & Virginia Woolf at The Hogarth Press, 52 Tavistock Square, London, W.C.1 1928
THE HOGARTH ESSAYS, SECOND SERIES, NO. 16
§ Buff paper wrappers printed in brown.
52 pp. (3) $6\frac{5}{8}$ x $4\frac{1}{8}$.
Published October 1928; number of copies not known.

178. **Snaith, Stanley** *A Flying Scroll* Printed and Published by Leonard and Virginia Woolf at The Hogarth Press, 52 Tavistock Square, London, W.C. 1928
§ Decorated yellow paper-covered boards; yellow label printed in black.
24 pp. (1) $7\frac{1}{2}$ x 5.
Published June 1928; number of copies not known.

179. **Thompson, Edward** *Cock Robin's Decease An Irregular Inquest* Published by Leonard & Virginia Woolf at The Hogarth Press, 52 Tavistock Square, London, W.C.1 1928
THE HOGARTH ESSAYS, SECOND SERIES, NO. 13
§ Grey paper wrappers printed in red.
75 pp. (3) $6\frac{5}{8}$ x $4\frac{1}{8}$.
Published March 1928; number of copies not known.

180. **Wellesley, Dorothy** *Matrix* Published by Leonard & Virginia Woolf at The Hogarth Press, 52 Tavistock Square, London, W.C.1 1928

HOGARTH LIVING POETS, FIRST SERIES, NO. 3

§ Blue-grey paper boards printed in black.
30 pp. (3) $7\frac{1}{2}$ x 5.
Published May 1928; 500 copies printed.

181. **White, Eric Walter** *Parnassus to Let An Essay about Rhythm in the Films* Published by Leonard & Virginia Woolf at The Hogarth Press, 52 Tavistock Square, London, W.C.1 1928

THE HOGARTH ESSAYS, SECOND SERIES, NO. 14

§ Buff paper wrappers printed in brown.
48 pp. (3) $6\frac{5}{8}$ x $4\frac{1}{8}$.
Published October 1928; 1,000 copies printed.

182. **Wilson, Florence** *Near East Educational Survey Report of a survey made during the months of April, May and June 1927* Published for the European Centre of the Carnegie Endowment for International Peace by the Hogarth Press 1928

§ Red paper wrappers printed in black.
108 pp. (3) $8\frac{1}{4}$ x $5\frac{1}{2}$.
Published August 1928; 1,500 copies printed.

183. **Wilson, Florence** *The Origins of the League Covenant Documentary History of its Drafting* With an Introduction by Professor P. J. Noel Baker. Issued under the auspices of The Association for International Understanding 10 St. James's Square, London, S.W.1 Published by Leonard and Virginia Woolf at The Hogarth Press, 52 Tavistock Square, London, W.C. 1928

§ Beige cloth printed in gilt. Dust wrapper not seen.
260 pp. (2) $8\frac{3}{4}$ x $5\frac{1}{2}$.
Published June 1928; 750 copies printed.

184. **Woolf, Leonard** *Imperialism and Civilization* Published by Leonard and Virginia Woolf at The Hogarth Press, 52 Tavistock Square, London 1928

§ Brown cloth printed in gilt. White dust wrapper printed in black.
135 pp. (2) $7\frac{3}{8}$ x $4\frac{7}{8}$.
Published March 1928; number of copies not known.

185. **Woolf, Virginia** *Orlando A Biography* Published by Leonard and Virginia Woolf at the Hogarth Press, 52 Tavistock Square, London, W.C. 1928
§ Orange cloth printed in gilt. White dust wrapper printed in black (see note).
299 pp. (2) $8\frac{5}{8}$ x $5\frac{1}{2}$.
Published October 1928; 5,080 copies printed.
NOTE: There is a variant binding, brown cloth.

1929

186. **Benkard, Ernst** *Undying Faces* A Collection of Death Masks With a Note by Georg Kolbe. Translated from the German by Margaret M. Green. Published by Leonard and Virginia Woolf at The Hogarth Press, 52 Tavistock Square, London, W.C.1 1929
§ Wine-colored paper boards, tan buckram spine printed in gilt. Blue dust wrapper printed in black.
118 pp. plus 112 plates (2) 10 x $6\frac{1}{2}$.
Published June 1929; 1,062 copies printed.

187. **Benson, Wilfrid** *The Foreigner in the Family* Published by Leonard and Virginia Woolf at the Hogarth Press, 52 Tavistock Square, London, W.C. 1929
§ Orange cloth printed in gilt. Orange dust wrapper printed in black.
219 pp. (2) $7\frac{1}{2}$ x 5.
Published June 1929; number of copies not known.

188. **Blunden, Edmund** *Nature in English Literature* Published by Leonard & Virginia Woolf at The Hogarth Press, 52 Tavistock Square, London, W.C.1 1929
HOGARTH LECTURES ON LITERATURE, FIRST SERIES, NO. 9
§ Orange cloth printed in red. Orange dust wrapper printed in red.
156 pp. (3) $7\frac{1}{2}$ x $4\frac{7}{8}$.
Published June 1929; 3,000 copies printed.

189. *Cambridge Poetry 1929* Edited by Christopher Saltmarshe, John Davenport & Basil Wright. Published by Leonard & Virginia Woolf at The Hogarth Press, 52 Tavistock Square, London, W.C.1 1929

§ Blue-grey paper boards printed in black.
76 pp. (3) $7\frac{1}{2}$ x 5.
Published March 1929; number of copies not known.
NOTE: Erratum slip loosely inserted.

190. **Cole, G. D. H.** *Politics and Literature* Published by Leonard & Virginia Woolf àt The Hogarth Press, 52 Tavistock Square, London, W.C.1 1929

HOGARTH LECTURES ON LITERATURE, FIRST SERIES, NO. 11
§ Orange cloth printed in red. Orange dust wrapper printed in red.
160 pp. (8) $7\frac{1}{2}$ x $4\frac{7}{8}$.

Published October 1929; 2,500 copies printed.

191. **Day Lewis, C.** *Transitional Poem* Published by Leonard & Virginia Woolf at The Hogarth Press, 52 Tavistock Square, London, W.C.1 1929

HOGARTH LIVING POETS, FIRST SERIES, NO. 9
§ Blue-green paper boards printed in blue.
71 pp. (3) $7\frac{1}{2}$ x 5.
Published October 1929; number of copies not known.

192. **Dutt, G. S.** *A Woman of India. Being the Life of Saroj Nalini (Founder of the Women's Institute Movement in India)* By Her Husband G.S. Dutt. (Introduction by C.F. Andrews). With a Foreword by Rabindranath Tagore. Published by Leonard & Virginia Woolf at The Hogarth Press, 52 Tavistock Square, London, W.C.1 1929
§ Green cloth printed in black. Dust wrapper not seen (see note).
144 pp. (3) $7\frac{1}{2}$ x $4\frac{7}{8}$.
Published May 1929; number of copies not known.
NOTE: Also issued in green paper wrappers printed in black. First published in Bengali in 1926.

193. **Graves, Ida** *The China Cupboard and Other Poems* Published by Leonard & Virginia Woolf at The Hogarth Press, 52 Tavistock Square, London, W.C.1 1929
HOGARTH LIVING POETS, FIRST SERIES, NO. 5
§ Blue-grey paper boards printed in black.
68 pp. (3) $7\frac{1}{2}$ x 5.
Published March 1929; number of copies not known.

194. Hewitt, Thos. J. & Ralph Hill *An Outline of Musical History Vol. I From the Earliest times to Handel and Bach by Thos. J. Hewitt; Vol. II From C. P. E. Bach to Modern Music by Ralph Hill* Published by Leonard and Virginia Woolf at The Hogarth Press, 52 Tavistock Square, London, W.C.1 1929 (2 volumes)

§ Buff cloth wrappers printed in black.

98 pp. and 146 pp. (5) $7\frac{1}{8}$ x $4\frac{3}{4}$.

Published October 1929; 2,000 copies printed.

NOTE: Also issued as two volumes bound in one; buff cloth printed in black and measuring $7\frac{3}{8}$ x $4\frac{1}{4}$.
Volume II was reportedly reprinted in 1931 but I haven't seen a copy.

195. Innes, Kathleen E. *The Reign of Law A Short and Simple Introduction to the Work of the Permanent Court of International Justice* Published by Leonard and Virginia Woolf at The Hogarth Press, 52 Tavistock Square, London, W.C.1 1929

§ Orange cloth wrappers printed in black.

42 pp. (5) $7\frac{1}{4}$ x $4\frac{7}{8}$.

Published November 1929; 2,000 copies printed.

196. Jeffers, Robinson *Cawdor* Published by Leonard & Virginia Woolf at The Hogarth Press, 52 Tavistock Square, London, W.C.1 1929

HOGARTH LIVING POETS, FIRST SERIES, NO. 12

§ Orange paper boards printed in black.

160 pp. (6) $8\frac{1}{4}$ x $5\frac{1}{4}$.

Published October 1929; 500 copies issued.

197. Kellett, E. E. *The Whirligig of Taste* Published by Leonard & Virginia Woolf at The Hogarth Press, 52 Tavistock Square, London, W.C.1 1929

HOGARTH LECTURES ON LITERATURE, FIRST SERIES, NO. 8

§ Orange cloth printed in red. Orange dust wrapper printed in red.

160 pp. (3) $7\frac{1}{2}$ x $4\frac{7}{8}$.

Published April 1929; 2,250 copies printed.

198. Kellett, E. E. *The Northern Saga* Published by Leonard and Virginia Woolf at the Hogarth Press, 52 Tavistock Square, London, W.C. 1929

§ Brown cloth printed in gilt. Blue-green dust wrapper printed in black.
205 pp. (2) $7\frac{1}{2}$ x $4\frac{7}{8}$.
Published September 1929; number of copies not known.

199. **Kitchin, C. H. B.** *Death of my Aunt* Published by Leonard and Virginia Woolf at the Hogarth Press, 52 Tavistock Square, London, W.C. 1929
§ Red cloth printed in gilt. White dust wrapper printed in green, black, and red.
248 pp. (2) $7\frac{1}{2}$ x $4\frac{7}{8}$.
Published September 1929; number of copies not known.

200. **Lucas, F. L.** *Time and Memory* Published by Leonard & Virginia Woolf at The Hogarth Press, 52 Tavistock Square, London, W.C.1 1929
HOGARTH LIVING POETS, FIRST SERIES, NO. 7
§ Blue-grey paper boards printed in black.
86 pp. (3) $7\frac{1}{2}$ x 5.
Published March 1929; 500 copies printed.

201. **Menai, Huw** *The Passing of Guto and Other Poems* Published by Leonard & Virginia Woolf at The Hogarth Press, 52 Tavistock Square, London, W.C.1 1929
HOGARTH LIVING POETS, FIRST SERIES, NO. 6
§ Blue-grey paper boards printed in black.
100 pp. (3) $7\frac{1}{2}$ x 5.
Published March 1929; number of copies not known.

202. **Montaigne, (Michel de)** *The Diary of Montaigne's Journey to Italy in 1580 and 1581* Translated with Introduction and Notes by E. J. Trechmann. Published by Leonard and Virginia Woolf at the Hogarth Press, 52 Tavistock Square, London, W.C. 1929
§ Green cloth printed in gilt. Dust wrapper not seen.
297 pp. (2) $8\frac{3}{4}$ x $5\frac{1}{2}$.
Month of publication not known; 1,050 copies printed.

203. **Norman, Sylva** *Nature Has No Tune* Published by Leonard and Virginia Woolf at the Hogarth Press, 52 Tavistock Square, London, W.C. 1929
§ Green cloth printed in gilt.   White dust wrapper printed in green.
358 pp. (23) $7\frac{1}{2}$ x 5.
Published September 1929; number of copies not known.

204. **Olivier, Lord** *White Capital & Coloured Labour* New Edition, Rewritten and Revised. Published by Leonard & Virginia Woolf at The Hogarth Press, 52 Tavistock Square, London 1929
§ Brown cloth printed in gilt.   White dust wrapper printed in black.
348 pp. (3) $8\frac{5}{8}$ x $5\frac{1}{2}$.
Published April 1929; 1,215 copies printed.
NOTE: Originally published in 1906 in *The Socialist Library*.

205. **Plomer, William** *Paper Houses* Published by Leonard and Virginia Woolf at the Hogarth Press, 52 Tavistock Square, London, W.C. 1929
§ Blue cloth printed in gilt.   Off-white dust wrapper printed in dark blue.
364 pp. (2) $7\frac{1}{2}$ x $4\frac{7}{8}$.
Published February 1929; 1,262 copies printed.

206. **Plomer, William** *The Family Tree* Published by Leonard & Virginia Woolf at The Hogarth Press, 52 Tavistock Square, London, W.C.1 1929
HOGARTH LIVING POETS, FIRST SERIES, NO. 10
§ Red paper boards printed in black.
106 pp. (3) $7\frac{1}{2}$ x 5.
Published October 1929; 400 copies printed.

207. **Sackville-West, V.** *King's Daughter* Published by Leonard & Virginia Woolf at The Hogarth Press, 52 Tavistock Square, London, W.C.1 1929
HOGARTH LIVING POETS, FIRST SERIES, NO. 11
§ Blue paper boards printed in black.
41 pp. (3) $7\frac{1}{2}$ x 5.
Published October 1929; 1,000 copies printed.
NOTE: Issued with an orange paper wrap-around band "By the Author of *The Land* which was awarded the Hawthornden Prize This is her latest book of poems since *The Land*."

208. **Starr, Mark** *Lies and Hate in Education* Published by Leonard and Virginia Woolf at the Hogarth Press, 52 Tavistock Square, London, W.C. 1929
§ Grey cloth printed in orange. Dust wrapper not seen (see note).
197 pp. (19) $7\frac{1}{2}$ x $4\frac{7}{8}$.
Published October 1929; number of copies not known.
NOTE: Also issued in green paper wrappers.

209. **Stephens, John S.** *Danger Zones of Europe A Study of National Minorities* Published by Leonard & Virginia Woolf at The Hogarth Press, 52 Tavistock Square, London, W.C.1 1929
THIRD MERTTENS LECTURE ON WAR AND PEACE
§ Blue cloth printed in black. Dust wrapper not seen.
86 pp. (3) $7\frac{3}{8}$ x $4\frac{7}{8}$.
Published June 1929; number of copies not known.

210. **Svevo, Italo** *The Hoax* Translated from the Italian, with an Introduction by Beryl de Zoete. Published by Leonard and Virginia Woolf at the Hogarth Press, 52 Tavistock Square, London, W.C. 1929
§ Red marbled cloth; white label on spine printed in red. Yellow dust wrapper printed in red.
151 pp. (2) $6\frac{3}{4}$ x $4\frac{1}{8}$.
Published October 1929; 1,000 copies printed.

211. **Wells, H. G.** *The Common Sense of World Peace* An Address Delivered in the Reichstag at Berlin, on Monday, April 15th, 1929. Published by Leonard & Virginia Woolf at The Hogarth Press, 52 Tavistock Square, London, W.C.1 1929
§ Blue paper boards; grey cloth spine; white label on spine printed in blue. White dust wrapper printed in black.
52 pp. (8) $7\frac{1}{2}$ x 5.
Published May 1929; 3,000 copies printed.

212. **Wolfe, Humbert** *Notes on English Verse Satire* Published by Leonard & Virginia Woolf at The Hogarth Press, 52 Tavistock Square, London, W.C.1 1929

HOGARTH LECTURES ON LITERATURE, FIRST SERIES, NO. 10

§ Orange cloth printed in red. Orange dust wrapper printed in red.
158 pp. (8) $7\frac{1}{2}$ x $4\frac{7}{8}$.
Published October 1929; 3,057 copies printed.

213. **Woolf, Virginia** *The Voyage Out* Published by Leonard & Virginia Woolf at The Hogarth Press, 52 Tavistock Square, London, 1929 Third Impression.

§ Jade green cloth printed in gilt. Dust wrapper not seen.
380 pp. (6) $7\frac{1}{2}$ x $5\frac{1}{8}$.
Published March or April 1929; 500 copies issued (400 pulped in September 1932).

NOTE: First Hogarth Press edition. The Hogarth Press bought the rights to this, Virginia's first book, in 1929, taking over 500 sets of sheets that Duckworth had imported from the George H. Doran Company, New York, and issuing them as the third impression with a cancel title page. The Hogarth Press issued a photo-offset edition as the first volume in the Uniform Edition of Virginia Woolf's works in September 1929.

214. **Woolf, Virginia** *Night and Day* Published by Leonard & Virginia Woolf at The Hogarth Press, Tavistock Square, London, 1929 Third Impression.

§ Hyacinth-blue cloth printed in gilt. Dust wrapper not seen.
540 pp. (32) $7\frac{3}{8}$ x $4\frac{7}{8}$.
Published March or April 1929; 667 copies issued.

NOTE: First Hogarth Press edition. The Hogarth Press bought the rights to this book in 1929, taking over 667 sets of sheets from Duckworth, and issuing them as the third impression with a cancel title page. The Hogarth Press issued a photo-offset edition in the Uniform Edition in November 1930.

215A. **Woolf, Virginia** *A Room of One's Own* New York The Fountain Press London The Hogarth Press 1929

§ Maroon cloth printed in gilt. Dust wrapper not seen.
161 pp. (6) $9\frac{5}{8}$ x $5\frac{5}{8}$.
Published October 1929 (see note).

NOTE: First (limited) edition.
Limited to 492 numbered and signed copies; the first one hundred copies for sale by The Hogarth Press in England, the balance for sale by Random House in America.

215B. **Woolf, Virginia** *A Room of One's Own* Published by Leonard and Virginia Woolf at the Hogarth Press, 52 Tavistock Square, London, W.C. 1929
§ Cinnanon cloth printed in gilt. Pale pink dust wrapper printed in navy blue.
172 pp. (2) 7 x $4\frac{1}{2}$.
Published October 1929; 3,040 copies printed.
NOTE: First (trade) edition.

216. **Benson, Wilfrid** *Dawn on Mont Blanc Being incidentally the tragedy of an aggravating young man* Published by Leonard and Virginia Woolf at the Hogarth Press, 52 Tavistock Square, London, W.C. 1930
§ Yellow cloth printed in gilt. Pink dust wrapper printed in purple.
368 pp. (2) $7\frac{1}{2}$ x $4\frac{7}{8}$.
Published February 1930; number of copies not known.

217. **Benson, Wilfrid** *As You Were* Published by Leonard & Virginia Woolf at The Hogarth Press, 52 Tavistock Square, London, W.C. 1930
§ Blue cloth printed in gilt. Cream dust wrapper printed in dark and light blue.
238 pp. (2) $7\frac{3}{8}$ x $4\frac{7}{8}$.
Published October 1930; number of copies not known.
NOTE: Not to be confused with *As We Were. A Victorian Peep-Show* by E. F. Benson, also published in London in 1930, but by a different publisher.

218. **Birrell, Francis & F. L. Lucas, Editors** *The Art of Dying An Anthology* Published by Leonard & Virginia Woolf at the Hogarth Press, 52 Tavistock Square, London, W.C.1 1930
§ Black cloth printed in gilt. Dust wrapper not seen.
96 pp. (3) $7\frac{1}{2}$ x $4\frac{7}{8}$.
Published November 1930; number of copies not known.

219. *Cambridge Poetry 1930* Edited by John Davenport, Hugh Sykes & Michael Redgrave.   Published by Leonard & Virginia Woolf at The Hogarth Press, 52 Tavistock Square, London, W.C.1 1930

HOGARTH LIVING POETS, FIRST SERIES, NO. 13

§ Pinkish tan paper boards printed in black.
71 pp. (3) $7\frac{1}{2}$ × 5.
Published May 1930; 800 copies printed.

220. **Dobb, Maurice** *Russia To-Day and To-Morrow* Published by Leonard and Virginia Woolf at The Hogarth Press, 52 Tavistock Square, London, W.C. 1930

DAY TO DAY PAMPHLETS NO. 1

§ Mottled green paper wrappers printed in black.
48 pp. (21) $7\frac{1}{4}$ × $4\frac{3}{4}$.
Published October 1930; 1,500 copies printed.

221. **Flugel, J. C.**   *The Psychology of Clothes*   Published by Leonard & Virginia Woolf at the Hogarth Press, 52 Tavistock Square, London, W.C. and The Institute of Psycho-Analysis MCMXXX

THE INTERNATIONAL PSYCHO-ANALYTICAL LIBRARY NO. 18

§ Green cloth printed in gilt. Dust wrapper not seen.
257 pp. (2) $9\frac{5}{8}$ × $6\frac{1}{4}$.
Published November 1930; 1,012 copies printed.

222. **Fox, R. M.** *Drifting Men* Published by Leonard & Virginia Woolf at The Hogarth Press, 52 Tavistock Square, London, W.C.1 1930

§ Orange cloth printed in gilt. White dust wrapper printed in grey.
150 pp. (5) $7\frac{1}{2}$ × 5.
Published October 1930; 1,000 copies printed.

223. **Freud, Sigm(und)** *Civilization and its Discontents* Published by Leonard & Virginia Woolf at The Hogarth Press, 52 Tavistock Square, London, W.C. and The Institute of Psycho-Analysis MCMXXX

THE INTERNATIONAL PSYCHO-ANALYTICAL LIBRARY NO. 17

§ Green cloth printed in gilt. Grey dust wrapper printed in black.
144 pp. (2) $9\frac{5}{8}$ × $6\frac{1}{2}$.
Published July 1930; 1,860 copies printed.

224. **Graham, John W.**   *Britain & America*   Published by Leonard & Virginia Woolf at The Hogarth Press, 52 Tavistock Square, London, W.C.1

THE MERTTENS LECTURE 1930

§ Blue cloth printed in black.   Probably not issued in dust wrapper (see note).

134 pp. (3) $7\frac{1}{2}$ x 5.

Published May 1930; 1,500 copies printed.

NOTE: Also issued in blue paper wrappers printed in black, measuring $7\frac{1}{4}$ x $4\frac{7}{8}$.

225. **Hoyland, John S.**   *History as Direction*   Published by Leonard and Virginia Woolf at the Hogarth Press, 52 Tavistock Square, London, W.C. 1930

§ Blue cloth printed in gilt. Buff dust wrapper printed in red.

175 pp. (2) $7\frac{1}{2}$ x $4\frac{7}{8}$.

Published October 1930; 1,008 copies printed.

226. **Jeffers, Robinson**   *Dear Judas and Other Poems*   1930 London   The Hogarth Press

HOGARTH LIVING POETS, FIRST SERIES, NO. 15

§ Pinkish brown paper boards printed in black.

129 pp. (6) $8\frac{1}{4}$ x $5\frac{1}{4}$.

Published November 1930; 300 copies issued.

227. **Macleod, Norman**   *German Lyric Poetry*   Published by Leonard & Virginia Woolf at The Hogarth Press, 52 Tavistock Square, London, W.C.1 1930

HOGARTH LECTURES ON LITERATURE, FIRST SERIES, NO. 13

§ Orange cloth printed in red. Orange dust wrapper printed in red.

158 pp. (8) $7\frac{1}{2}$ x $4\frac{7}{8}$.

Published October 1930; 2,545 copies printed.

228. **Mann, F. O.**   *St. James's Park and other poems*   Published by Leonard & Virginia Woolf at The Hogarth Press, 52 Tavistock Square, London, W.C.1 1930

§ Orange paper wrappers; cream label printed in black.

102 pp. (3) $7\frac{1}{2}$ x 5.

Published February 1930; number of copies not known.

229. **Money-Kyrle, R.** *The Meaning of Sacrifice* Thesis Approved for the Degree of Doctor of Philosophy in the University of London. Published by Leonard & Virginia Woolf at The Hogarth Press, 52 Tavistock Square, London, W.C. and The Institute of Psycho-Analysis MCMXXX

THE INTERNATIONAL PSYCHO-ANALYTICAL LIBRARY NO. 16

§ Green cloth printed in gilt. Dust wrapper not seen. 273 pp. (2) $9\frac{5}{8}$ x $6\frac{1}{4}$.

Published May 1930, 750 copies printed.

230. **Palmer, Herbert E.** *The Armed Muse Poems* Published by Leonard & Virginia Woolf at The Hogarth Press, 52 Tavistock Square, London, W.C.1 1930

§ Green paper boards; light green paper label printed in black.

44 pp. (5) $7\frac{1}{2}$ x 5.

Published October 1930; number of copies not known.

231. **Racine, Louis** *Life of Milton Together with Observations on* PARADISE LOST Translated with an Introduction by Katherine John. Published by Leonard and Virginia Woolf at the Hogarth Press, 52 Tavistock Square, London, W.C. 1930

§ Red cloth printed in gilt. Grey dust wrapper printed in blue.

158 pp. (2) $7\frac{1}{2}$ x 5.

Published October 1930; 1,000 copies printed.

232. **Rilke, Rainer Maria** *The Notebook of Malte Laurids Brigge* Translated by John Linton. Published by Leonard and Virginia Woolf The Hogarth Press, Tavistock Square MCMXXX (1931)

§ Green cloth printed in gilt. Dust wrapper not seen. 243 pp. (6) $7\frac{3}{8}$ x $4\frac{7}{8}$.

Published February 1931; 1,050 copies printed.

233. **Ritchie, Alice** *Occupied Territory* Published by Leonard and Virginia Woolf at The Hogarth Press, 52 Tavistock Square, W.C.1 1930

§ Olive-green cloth printed in gilt. White dust wrapper printed in dark grey.
240 pp. (8) 7½ x 4⅞.
Published March 1930; number of copies not known.

234. **Robinson, Edwin Arlington** *Cavender's House* Published by Leonard & Virginia Woolf at The Hogarth Press, 52 Tavistock Square, London, W.C.1 1930
HOGARTH LIVING POETS, FIRST SERIES, NO. 14
§ Lavender paper boards printed in black.
67 pp. (3) 7½ x 5.
Published April 1930; number of copies not known.

235A. **Sackville-West, V.** *The Edwardians* Published by Leonard & Virginia Woolf The Hogarth Press, Tavistock Square 1930
§ Red cloth; vellum spine printed in gilt. Not issued in dust wrapper.
349 pp. (2) 7¾ x 5.
Published May 1930; 125 numbered and signed copies.
NOTE: First (limited) edition.

235B. **Sackville-West, V.** *The Edwardians* Published by Leonard & Virginia Woolf The Hogarth Press, Tavistock Square 1930
§ Orange cloth printed in gilt. Peach-colored dust wrapper printed in black.
349 pp. (2) 7½ x 4⅞.
Published May 1930; 3,030 copies printed.
NOTE: First (trade) edition.

236. **Samuel, Horace B.** *Unholy. Memories of the Holy Land* Published by Leonard and Virginia Woolf at The Hogarth Press, 52 Tavistock Square, London, W.C.1 1930
§ Grey cloth printed in gilt. White dust wrapper printed in black.
314 pp. (19) 8⅝ x 5½.
Published March 1930; 1,000 copies printed.

237. **Samuel, Horace B.** *Beneath the Whitewash   A critical analysis of the report of the Commission on the Palestine Disturbances of August, 1929*   Published by Leonard and Virginia Woolf at the Hogarth Press   52, Tavistock Square, W.C.1   1930
§ Brown paper wrappers printed in black.
50 pp. (13) $8\frac{1}{2}$ x $5\frac{1}{2}$.
Published June 1930; number of copies not known.

238. **Schonfield, Hugh J., Editor**   *Letters to Frederick Tennyson*   Published by Leonard and Virginia Woolf at The Hogarth Press, 52 Tavistock Square, London, W.C.   1930
§ Green cloth printed in gilt.   Dust wrapper not seen.
146 pp. (2) $8\frac{5}{8}$ x $5\frac{1}{2}$.
Published October 1930; number of copies not known.

239. **Svevo, Italo**   *The Nice Old Man and the Pretty Girl and other stories*   Translated from the Italian by L. Collison-Morley. Published by Leonard and Virginia Woolf at The Hogarth Press, 52 Tavistock Square, London, W.C.   1930
§ Orange cloth printed in gilt.   Cream dust wrapper printed in red.
162 pp. (2) $7\frac{1}{2}$ x 5.
Published November 1930; 1,000 copies printed.
NOTE: Introductory Note by Eugenio Montale.

240. **Vines, Sherard**   *The Course of English Classicism From the Tudor to the Victorian Age*   Published by Leonard & Virginia Woolf at The Hogarth Press, 52 Tavistock Square, London, W.C.1   1930
HOGARTH LECTURES ON LITERATURE, FIRST SERIES, NO. 12
§ Orange cloth printed in red.   Orange dust wrapper printed in red.
160 pp. (8) $7\frac{1}{2}$ x $4\frac{7}{8}$.
Published February 1930; number of copies not known.

241. **Wellesley, Dorothy**   *Deserted House   A Poem-Sequence*   Published by Leonard & Virginia Woolf at The Hogarth Press, 52 Tavistock Square, London, W.C.1   1930
HOGARTH LIVING POETS, FIRST SERIES, NO. 16
§ Green paper boards printed in black.
80 pp. (3) $7\frac{1}{2}$ x 5.
Published November 1930; number of copies not known.

242. **Wellesley, Dorothy, Editor**   *A Broadcast Anthology of Modern Poetry*   Published by Leonard & Virginia Woolf at The Hogarth Press, 52 Tavistock Square, London, W.C.1 1930

HOGARTH LIVING POETS, FIRST SERIES, NO. 17

§ Lavender paper boards printed in black.

238 pp. (3) $7\frac{1}{2}$ x 5.

Published November 1930; 2,130 copies printed.

243. **Wells, H. G.**   *The Open Conspiracy   Blue Prints for a World Revolution   A Second Version of this faith of a modern man made more explicit and plain*   Published by Leonard and Virginia Woolf at The Hogarth Press, 52 Tavistock Square, London, W.C.1 1930

§ Blue paper boards; grey cloth spine; white label on spine printed in blue. Pink dust wrapper printed in blue.

243 pp. (8) $7\frac{1}{2}$ x 5.

Published February 1930; number of copies not known.

NOTE: Second edition with a new Preface and some new matter. Originally published by Victor Gollancz in 1928.

244. **White, Eric Walter**   *Stravinsky's Sacrifice to Apollo*   Published by Leonard and Virginia Woolf at the Hogarth Press, 52 Tavistock Square, London, W.C. 1930

§ Orange cloth printed in gilt.   Green dust wrapper printed in black.

150 pp. (2) $7\frac{1}{2}$ x 5.

Published May 1930; 1,000 copies printed.

245. **Woolf, Virginia**   *On Being Ill*   Printed and published by Leonard & Virginia Woolf at The Hogarth Press   1930

§ Pale blue-green cloth;   vellum spine printed in gilt. White dust wrapper printed in grey, black, and yellow.

35 pp. (1) 8 x $5\frac{1}{8}$.

Published November 1930; limited to 250 numbered and signed copies plus about 25 "out of series" copies.

NOTE: B. J. Kirkpatrick, in *A Bibliography of Virginia Woolf* (Second edition, revised, Rupert Hart-Davis, 1967), mentions a preliminary state in which the printed limitation is 125 and is printed over with a line and the figure 250 inserted. "Out of series" was recorded in purple ink by Mr. Woolf in place of a number. This preliminary state, according to Mr. Woolf, comprised about 25 copies which were distributed free, probably without dust wrappers. For what it may be worth, I have seen copy number 250, which had the limitation changed as above and was in dust wrapper.

246. **Bevan, Aneurin, M. P., E. J. Strachey, M. P., George Strauss, M. P.** *What We Saw in Russia* Published by Leonard and Virginia Woolf at The Hogarth Press, 52 Tavistock Square, London, W.C. 1931

DAY TO DAY PAMPHLETS NO. 4

§ Yellow paper wrappers printed in black.

30 pp. (21) $7\frac{1}{4}$ x $4\frac{3}{4}$.

Publication date and number of copies printed not known.

247. **Buxton, Charles Roden, M. P.** *The Race Problem in Africa* Published by Leonard & Virginia Woolf at The Hogarth Press, 52 Tavistock Square, London, W.C.1

THE MERTTENS LECTURE 1931

§ Blue cloth printed in black. Dust wrapper not seen.

60 pp. (3) $7\frac{3}{8}$ x $4\frac{3}{4}$.

Published May 1931; 1,500 copies printed.

NOTE: Also issued in blue paper wrappers printed in black.

248. *Cambridge Women's Verse, An Anthology of* Compiled by Margaret Thomas. Published by Leonard & Virginia Woolf at The Hogarth Press, 52 Tavistock Square, London, W.C.1 1931

HOGARTH LIVING POETS, FIRST SERIES, NO. 20

§ Buff paper boards printed in black.

56 pp. (3) $7\frac{1}{2}$ x 5.

Published February 1931; number of copies not known.

249. **Cecil, Viscount** *A Letter to an M. P. on Disarmament* Published by Leonard & Virginia Woolf at The Hogarth Press, 52 Tavistock Square, London, W.C.1 1931

THE HOGARTH LETTERS NO. 2

§ Cream paper wrappers printed in grey and black.

40 pp. (5) $7\frac{3}{8}$ x $4\frac{3}{4}$.

Month of publication not known; 5,000 copies printed.

250. **Davies, Margaret Llewelyn, Editor** *Life as we have known it By Co-Operative working women* With an Introductory Letter by Virginia Woolf. Published by Leonard and Virginia Woolf at The Hogarth Press, 52 Tavistock Square, London, W.C. 1931

§ Yellow cloth printed in black. White dust wrapper printed in black.
141 pp. (5) 7 $\frac{3}{8}$ x 4 $\frac{7}{8}$.
Published March 1931; 1,500 copies printed.

251. **Day Lewis, C.** *From Feathers to Iron* Published by Leonard & Virginia Woolf at The Hogarth Press, 52 Tavistock Square, London, W.C.1 1931
HOGARTH LIVING POETS, FIRST SERIES, NO. 22
§ Yellow paper boards printed in black.
58 pp. (3) 7 $\frac{1}{2}$ x 5.
Published September 1931; number of copies not known.

252. **Derwent, Lord** *Fifty Poems* Published by Leonard & Virginia Woolf at The Hogarth Press, 52 Tavistock Square, London, W.C.1 1931
HOGARTH LIVING POETS, FIRST SERIES, NO. 18
§ Buff paper boards printed in black.
87 pp. (3) 7 $\frac{1}{2}$ x 5.
Published February 1931; 500 copies printed.

253. **Easdale, Joan Adeney** *A Collection of Poems* (*Written between the ages of 14 and 17*) Published by Leonard & Virginia Woolf at The Hogarth Press, 52 Tavistock Square, London, W.C.1 1931
HOGARTH LIVING POETS, FIRST SERIES, NO. 19
§ Light red paper boards printed in black.
88 pp. (3) 7 $\frac{1}{2}$ x 5.
Published February 1931; number of copies not known.

254. **Forster, E. M.** *A Letter to Madan Blanchard* Published by Leonard & Virginia Woolf at The Hogarth Press, 52 Tavistock Square, London, W.C.1 1931
THE HOGARTH LETTERS NO. 1
§ Buff paper wrappers printed in black and blue.
27 pp. (5) 7 $\frac{3}{8}$ x 4 $\frac{3}{4}$.
Published October 1931; 5,000 copies printed of which 500 copies were bound up in the collected edition of *The Hogarth Letters*.

255. **Fraser, L. M.**   *Protection and Free Trade*   Published by Leonard and Virginia Woolf at The Hogarth Press, 52 Tavistock Square London, W.C. 1931

DAY TO DAY PAMPHLETS NO. 5

§ Blue paper wrappers printed in black.

52 pp. (17) $7\frac{1}{4}$ x $4\frac{3}{4}$.

Published September 1931; 2,000 copies printed.

256. **Hampson, John**   *Saturday Night at the Greyhound*   Published by Leonard and Virginia Woolf at The Hogarth Press, 52 Tavistock Square, London, W.C. 1931

§ Green cloth printed in gilt. White dust wrapper printed in dark blue.

242 pp. (2) $7\frac{1}{2}$ x $4\frac{7}{8}$.

Published February 1931; number of copies not known.
NOTE: John Hampson is a pseudonym for John Hampson Simpson.

257. **Havens, Allen**   *The Trap*   Published by Leonard and Virginia Woolf at The Hogarth Press, Tavistock Square, London 1931

§ Dark green cloth printed in gilt. Dust wrapper not seen.

656 pp. (2) $8\frac{3}{4}$ x $5\frac{1}{2}$.

Published September 1931; number of copies not known.
NOTE: Also bound, somewhat taller, in light green cloth.
Allen Havens is a pseudonym for Maud Allen.

258. **Ireland, Denis**   *Ulster To-Day and To-Morrow   Her Part in a Gaelic Civilization   A Study in Political Re-Evolution*   Published by Leonard and Virginia Woolf at The Hogarth Press, 52 Tavistock Square, London, W.C. 1931

DAY TO DAY PAMPHLETS NO. 6

§ Yellow paper wrappers printed in black.

56 pp. (17) $7\frac{1}{4}$ x $4\frac{3}{4}$.

Published September 1931; number of copies not known.

259. **Joad, C. E. M.**   *The Horrors of the Countryside*   Published by Leonard and Virginia Woolf at The Hogarth Press, 52 Tavistock Square, London, W.C. 1931

DAY TO DAY PAMPHLETS NO. 3

§ Green paper wrappers printed in black.

45 pp. (21) $7\frac{1}{4}$ x $4\frac{3}{4}$.

Published March 1931; number of copies not known.

260. **Jones, Ernest** *On the Nightmare* Published by Leonard & Virginia Woolf at The Hogarth Press, 52 Tavistock Square, London, W.C.1 and The Institute of Psycho-Analysis MCMXXXI
THE INTERNATIONAL PSYCHO-ANALYTICAL LIBRARY NO. 20
§ Green cloth printed in gilt. Dust wrapper not seen. 374 pp. (2) $8\frac{7}{8}$ x $5\frac{1}{2}$.
Published October 1931; 1,640 copies printed.

261. **Kitchin, C. H. B.** *The Sensitive One* Published by Leonard and Virginia Woolf at The Hogarth Press, 52 Tavistock Square, London, W.C. 1931
§ Grey cloth printed in gilt. Cream dust wrapper printed in blue.
181 pp. (2) $7\frac{1}{2}$ x 5.
Published February 1931; 1,200 copies printed.

262. **Lehmann, John** *A Garden Revisited and Other Poems* Published by Leonard & Virginia Woolf at The Hogarth Press, 52 Tavistock Square, London, W.C.1 1931
HOGARTH LIVING POETS, FIRST SERIES, NO. 21
§ Red paper boards printed in black.
52 pp. (3) $7\frac{1}{2}$ x 5.
Published September 1931; 400 copies printed.

263. **Lehmann, Rosamond** *A Letter to a Sister* Published by Leonard & Virginia Woolf at The Hogarth Press, 52 Tavistock Square, London, W.C.1 1931
THE HOGARTH LETTERS NO. 3
§ Cream paper wrappers printed in red and black.
24 pp. (5) $7\frac{3}{8}$ x $4\frac{3}{4}$.
Month of publication not known; 4,000 copies printed.

264. **Leys, Norman** *A Last Chance in Kenya* Published by Leonard and Virginia Woolf at The Hogarth Press, Tavistock Square, London 1931
§ Red cloth printed in gilt. Red dust wrapper printed in black.
173 pp. (2) 9 x $5\frac{3}{4}$.
Published December 1931; 1,500 copies printed.

265. **Macaulay, Rose** *Some Religious Elements in English Literature*
Published by Leonard & Virginia Woolf at The Hogarth
Press, 52 Tavistock Square, London, W.C.1 1931
HOGARTH LECTURES ON LITERATURE, FIRST SERIES, NO. 14
§ Orange cloth printed in red. Orange dust wrapper
printed in red.
160 pp. (8) $7\frac{1}{2}$ x $4\frac{7}{8}$.
Published May 1931; 3,000 copies printed.

266. **Plomer, William** *Sado* Published by Leonard and Virginia Woolf at The Hogarth Press, 52 Tavistock Square,
London, W.C. 1931
§ Orange cloth printed in blue. White dust wrapper
printed in blue.
274 pp. (2) $7\frac{1}{2}$ x $4\frac{7}{8}$.
Published September 1931; number of copies not known.

267. **Reik, Theodor** *Ritual Psycho-Analytic Studies* With a
Preface by Sigm. Freud. Translated from the Second
German Edition by Douglas Bryan. Published by Leon-
ard & Virginia Woolf at The Hogarth Press, 52 Tavistock
Square, London, W.C.1 and The Institute of Psycho-
Analysis 1931
THE INTERNATIONAL PSYCHO-ANALYTICAL LIBRARY NO. 19
§ Green cloth printed in gilt. Dust wrapper not seen.
367 pp. (2) $9\frac{5}{8}$ x $6\frac{1}{4}$.
Published June 1931; 1,000 copies printed of which 250
sets of sheets were exported to America.

268. **Rilke, Rainer Maria** *Duineser Elegien Elegies From the
Castle of Duino* Translated from the German of Rainer
Maria Rilke by V. Sackville-West and Edward Sackville
West.
§ Buff paper boards; vellum spine and corners; printed
in gilt.
134 pp. (4) 10 x 6.
Published October 1931; 238 numbered copies printed.
NOTE: The Hogarth Press imprint does not appear on the title page.
The following appears on the limitation page, "Count Harry Kess-
ler planned the format of this volume. Eric Gill designed and him-
self cut on wood the initials. The Italic type was designed by Edward
Johnston and cut by E. Prince and G. T. Friend. The paper was made
by a hand process devised in joint research by Count Harry Kessler

and Gaspard and Aristide Maillol. The book was printed in the winter and spring of 1931. Count Harry Kessler and Max Goertz supervised the work of setting the type and printing. Compositors: Walter Tanz and Hans Schulze. Pressman: Willi Laste. The book was printed for The Hogarth Press, 52 Tavistock Square, London W. C. 1, and both the English and the German texts were reproduced by the courtesy of Insel-Verlag in Leipzig who are also the agents for the book in Germany.

"The whole edition consists of two hundred and thirty numbered copies for sale on handmade Maillol-Kessler paper with the watermark of the Cranach Press, and signed by the translators; and eight numbered copies on vellum for sale with hand-gilded initials, signed by the translators. This is copy nr."

269. **Rylands, George** *Poems* Printed & published by L. & V. Woolf at The Hogarth Press, London. 1931

§ Light green paper boards, dark green and brown herringbone design; white paper label printed in black. Plain tissue dust wrapper.

Unpaginated (1) 7 x $4\frac{1}{2}$.

Published December 1931; limited to 350 numbered and signed copies.

270. **Sackville-West, V.** *All Passion Spent* Published by Leonard and Virginia Woolf at The Hogarth Press, Tavistock Square, London 1931

§ Blue-green cloth printed in gilt. Cream dust wrapper printed in mauve and purple.

297 pp. (2) $7\frac{3}{8}$ x $4\frac{7}{8}$.

Published May 1931; 4,040 copies printed.

271. **Sackville-West, V.** *Sissinghurst* Printed by hand by Leonard & Virginia Woolf and published at The Hogarth Press, London. 1931

§ Brown marbled paper boards printed in dark brown. Unpaginated (1) $8\frac{5}{8}$ x $6\frac{7}{8}$.

Published July 1931; limited to 500 numbered and signed copies.

272. **Stewart, Jean** *Poetry in France and England* Published by Leonard & Virginia Woolf at The Hogarth Press, 52 Tavistock Square, London, W.C.1 1931

HOGARTH LECTURES ON LITERATURE, FIRST SERIES, NO. 15

§ Orange cloth printed in red. Orange dust wrapper printed in red.

160 pp. (8) $7\frac{1}{2}$ x $4\frac{7}{8}$.

Published May 1931; 2,750 copies printed of which 250 sets of sheets were sent to Harcourt, Brace in America.

273. **Trevelyan, R. C.** *Three Plays Sulla, Fand, The Pearl-Tree*
Published by Leonard & Virginia Woolf at The Hogarth
Press, 52 Tavistock Square, London, W.C.1 1931
§ Brown-gold marbled paper boards; white paper label
printed in black.
120 pp. (3) $7\frac{3}{8}$ x $4\frac{3}{4}$.
Published May 1931; 500 copies printed.

274. **Trouton, Rupert** *Unemployment Its Causes and Their
Remedies* With a Foreword by J. M. Keynes. Published
by Leonard and Virginia Woolf at The Hogarth Press,
52 Tavistock Square, London, W.C. 1931
DAY TO DAY PAMPHLETS NO. 2
§ Mottled green paper wrappers printed in black.
52 pp. (21) $7\frac{1}{4}$ x $4\frac{3}{4}$.
Published March 1931; 2,000 copies printed.

275. **White, Eric Walter** *Walking Shadows An Essay on Lotte
Reiniger's Silhouette Films* Published by Leonard and Vir-
ginia Woolf at The Hogarth Press, 52 Tavistock Square
London W.C.1
§ White paper boards printed in black.
31 pp. (17) $7\frac{1}{2}$ x 5.
Publication date and number of copies printed not known.

276. **Wise, Marjorie** *English Village Schools* Published by
Leonard & Virginia Woolf at The Hogarth Press, 52
Tavistock Square, London, W.C.1 1931
§ Orange cloth printed in blue. Buff dust wrapper
printed in orange.
159 pp. (5) $7\frac{3}{8}$ x $4\frac{7}{8}$.
Published September 1931; 1,000 copies printed.

277. **Woolf, Leonard** *The Village in the Jungle* New Edition.
Published by Leonard & Virginia Woolf at the Hogarth
Press, London, W.C.1 1931
§ Green cloth printed in gilt. Dust wrapper not seen.
307 pp. (23) $7\frac{3}{8}$ x $4\frac{7}{8}$.
Published September 1931; 1,200 copies printed.
NOTE: Fifth edition, but first Hogarth Press edition.

278. **Woolf, Leonard** *After the Deluge   A Study in Communal Psychology*   Vol. I.   Published by Leonard and Virginia Woolf at The Hogarth Press, Tavistock Square, London 1931

§ Tan cloth printed in gilt.   Dust wrapper not seen.
347 pp. (2) $8\frac{1}{2}$ x $5\frac{1}{2}$.
Published October 1931; number of copies not known.
NOTE: Volume II was published in 1939 with the same title; Volume III was published in 1951 with the title *Principia Politica*.

279. **Woolf, Virginia** *The Waves* Published by Leonard and Virginia Woolf at The Hogarth Press, Tavistock Square, London 1931

§ Purple cloth printed in gilt.   Cream dust wrapper printed in lime-green and brown.
325 pp. (2) $7\frac{1}{2}$ x $4\frac{3}{4}$.
Published October 1931; 7,113 copies printed.

1 9 3 2

280. **Barnes, Leonard** *The New Boer War* Published by Leonard and Virginia Woolf at The Hogarth Press, 52 Tavistock Square, London, W.C.1 1932

§ Green cloth printed in black. Buff dust wrapper printed in orange.
238 pp. (5) $7\frac{3}{8}$ x 5.
Published October 1932; 1,250 copies printed.

281. **Birrell, Francis** *A Letter From a Black Sheep* Published by Leonard & Virginia Woolf at The Hogarth Press, 52 Tavistock Square, London, W.C.1   1932

THE HOGARTH LETTERS NO. 5

§ Cream paper wrappers printed in black and brown.
30 pp. (5) $7\frac{3}{8}$ x $4\frac{3}{4}$.
Published January 1932; 2,000 copies printed.

282. **Brailsford, Henry Noel** *If We Want Peace*   Published by Leonard and Virginia Woolf at The Hogarth Press, 52 Tavistock Square London W.C. for The New Fabian Research Bureau 1932

DAY TO DAY PAMPHLETS NO. 11

§ Blue paper wrappers printed in black.
64 pp. (5) $7\frac{1}{4}$ x $4\frac{3}{4}$.
Published July 1932; 2,000 copies printed.
NOTE: Also issued in cloth and dust wrapper but I haven't seen a copy.

283. **Charques, R. D.** *Soviet Education Some Aspects of Cultural Revolution* Published by Leonard and Virginia Woolf at The Hogarth Press, 52 Tavistock Square London W.C. 1932

DAY TO DAY PAMPHLETS NO. 12

§ Bright purple paper wrappers printed in black.

48 pp. (5) $7\frac{1}{4}$ x $4\frac{3}{4}$.

Published September 1932; number of copies not known.

284. **Deutsch, Dr. Helene** *Psycho-analysis of the Neuroses* Translated by W. D. Robson-Scott. Published by Leonard and Virginia Woolf at The Hogarth Press, Tavistock Square, London and The Institute of Psycho-Analysis 1932

THE INTERNATIONAL PSYCHO-ANALYTICAL LIBRARY NO. 23

§ Green cloth printed in gilt. Dust wrapper not seen.

237 pp. (2) $8\frac{1}{2}$ x $5\frac{1}{2}$.

Month of publication not known; 1,250 copies printed.

285. **Dobb, Maurice** *On Marxism To-Day* Published by Leonard and Virginia Woolf at The Hogarth Press, 52 Tavistock Square London W.C. 1932

DAY TO DAY PAMPHLETS NO. 10

§ Red paper wrappers printed in black.

48 pp. (5) $7\frac{1}{4}$ x $4\frac{3}{4}$.

Published April 1932; number of copies not known.

286. **Dobree, Bonamy** *St. Martin's Summer* Published by Leonard and Virginia Woolf at The Hogarth Press, Tavistock Square, London 1932

§ Blue cloth printed in red. Cream dust wrapper printed in sepia.

359 pp. (2) $7\frac{1}{2}$ x 5.

Published September 1932; number of copies not known.

287. **Easdale, Joan Adeney** *Clemence and Clare* Published by Leonard & Virginia Woolf at The Hogarth Press, 52 Tavistock Square, London, W.C.1 1932

HOGARTH LIVING POETS, FIRST SERIES, NO. 23

§ Yellow paper boards printed in black.

48 pp. (3) $7\frac{1}{2}$ x 5.

Published March 1932; 500 copies printed.

288. **Garratt, G. T.** *The Mugwumps and the Labour Party* Published by Leonard & Virginia Woolf at The Hogarth Press, 52 Tavistock Square, London, W.C.1 1932
§ Orange cloth printed in black. Cream dust wrapper printed in brown.
160 pp. (5) $7\frac{3}{8}$ x $4\frac{3}{4}$.
Published February 1932; 1,200 copies printed.

289. **Golding, Louis** *A Letter to Adolf Hitler* Published by Leonard & Virginia Woolf at The Hogarth Press, 52 Tavistock Square, London, W.C.1 1932
THE HOGARTH LETTERS NO. 11
§ Cream paper wrappers printed in black and rose.
28 pp. (5) $7\frac{3}{8}$ x $4\frac{3}{4}$.
Published October 1932; 2,500 copies printed.

290. **Hampson, John** *O Providence* Published by Leonard and Virginia Woolf at The Hogarth Press, Tavistock Square, London 1932
§ Grey cloth printed in black. White dust wrapper printed in blue-green.
394 pp. (2) $7\frac{3}{8}$ x $4\frac{7}{8}$.
Published February 1932; number of copies not known.
NOTE: John Hampson is a pseudonym for John Hampson Simpson.

291. **Hardwick, J. C.** *A Letter to an Archbishop* Published by Leonard & Virginia Woolf at The Hogarth Press, 52 Tavistock Square, London, W.C.1 1932
THE HOGARTH LETTERS NO. 10
§ Cream paper wrappers printed in black and yellow.
35 pp. (5) $7\frac{3}{8}$ x $4\frac{3}{4}$.
Published October 1932; 2,000 copies printed.

292. **Hobson, J. A.** *From Capitalism to Socialism* Published by Leonard and Virginia Woolf at The Hogarth Press, 52 Tavistock Square London W.C. 1932
DAY TO DAY PAMPHLETS NO. 8
§ Orange paper wrappers printed in black.
53 pp. (5) $7\frac{1}{4}$ x $4\frac{3}{4}$.
Published October 1932; number of copies not known.

293. **Irvine, Lyn Ll.** *Ten Letter-Writers* Published by Leonard and Virginia Woolf at The Hogarth Press, 52 Tavistock Square, London, W.C.1 1932
§ Green cloth printed in gilt. Cream dust wrapper printed in green.
230 pp. (5) $8\frac{5}{8}$ x $5\frac{1}{2}$.
Published September 1932; number of copies not known.

294. **Isherwood, Christopher** *The Memorial Portrait of a Family* Published by Leonard and Virginia Woolf at the Hogarth Press, 52 Tavistock Square, London, W.C. 1932
§ Rough (later smooth) red cloth printed in blue. Brown dust wrapper printed in blue.
294 pp. (2) $7\frac{1}{2}$ x $4\frac{5}{8}$.
Published February 1932; number of copies not known.

295. **Klein, Melanie** *The Psycho-Analysis of Children* Published by Leonard & Virginia Woolf at The Hogarth Press, 52 Tavistock Square, London, W.C. and The Institute of Psycho-Analysis 1932
THE INTERNATIONAL PSYCHO-ANALYTICAL LIBRARY NO. 22
§ Green cloth printed in gilt. Dust wrapper not seen.
393 pp. (2) $8\frac{1}{2}$ x $5\frac{1}{2}$.
Published November 1932; number of copies not known.

296. **Laforgue, René** *The Defeat of Baudelaire A Psycho-Analytical Study of the Neuroses of Charles Baudelaire* Published by Leonard and Virginia Woolf at The Hogarth Press, Tavistock Square, London 1932
THE INTERNATIONAL PSYCHO-ANALYTICAL LIBRARY NO. 21
§ Green cloth printed in gilt. Bright green dust wrapper printed in black.
192 pp. (2) $8\frac{3}{4}$ x $5\frac{5}{8}$.
Published February 1932; number of copies not known.

297. **Laski, Harold J.** *The Crisis and the Constitution: 1931 and After* Published by L. and V. Woolf at The Hogarth Press, 52 Tavistock Square, W.C.1 and by The Fabian Society at 11 Dartmouth Street, S.W.1 1932
DAY TO DAY PAMPHLETS NO. 9

§ Green paper wrappers printed in black.
64 pp. (5) $7\frac{1}{4}$ x $4\frac{3}{4}$.
Published February 1932; number of copies not known.
NOTE: Also issued in green cloth printed in gilt; green dust wrapper printed in black.

298. **Lloyd, C. M.** *Russian Notes* Published by Leonard & Virginia Woolf at The Hogarth Press, 52 Tavistock Square London, W.C. 1932
DAY TO DAY PAMPHLETS NO. 7
§ Orange paper wrappers printed in black.
40 pp. (5) $7\frac{1}{4}$ x $4\frac{3}{4}$.
Published February 1932; 2,000 copies printed.

299. **Mortimer, Raymond** *The French Pictures A Letter to Harriet* Published by Leonard & Virginia Woolf at The Hogarth Press, 52 Tavistock Square, London, W.C.1 1932
THE HOGARTH LETTERS NO. 4
§ Cream paper wrappers printed in orange and black.
31 pp. (5) $7\frac{3}{8}$ x $4\frac{3}{4}$.
Published January 1932; 2,500 copies printed.

300. **Pekin L. B.** *Public Schools Their Failure and Their Reform* Published by Leonard and Virginia Woolf at The Hogarth Press, 52 Tavistock Square, London, W.C. 1932
§ Brown cloth printed in blue. Buff dust wrapper printed in blue.
224 pp. (17) $7\frac{1}{4}$ x $4\frac{3}{4}$.
Published February 1932; number of copies not known.
NOTE: L. B. Pekin is a pseudonym for Reginald Snell.

301. **Plomer, William** *The Fivefold Screen* Published by Leonard and Virginia Woolf at The Hogarth Press, 52 Tavistock Square, London, W.C. 1932
§ Black cloth printed in gilt. Dust wrapper not seen.
63 pp. (2) $10\frac{1}{4}$ x $7\frac{1}{4}$.
Published May 1932; limited to 450 numbered and signed copies.

302. **Plomer, William** *The Case is Altered* Published by Leonard and Virginia Woolf at The Hogarth Press, Tavistock Square, London 1932
§ Green cloth printed in gilt. Grey dust wrapper printed in red.
341 pp. (2) $7\frac{1}{2}$ x $4\frac{7}{8}$.
Published July 1932; 1,520 copies printed.

303. **Pole, D. Graham** *India in Transition* With a Foreword by The Rt. Hon. Wedgwood Benn. Published by Leonard and Virginia Woolf at The Hogarth Press, 52 Tavistock Square, London, W.C.1 1932
§ Orange cloth printed in black. Buff dust wrapper printed in blue.
395 pp. (5) $7\frac{3}{8}$ x $4\frac{3}{4}$.
Published October 1932; number of copies not known.

304. **Ponsonby, Arthur** *Disarmament A Discussion* Published by Leonard and Virginia Woolf at The Hogarth Press, 52 Tavistock Square London W.C. 1932
DAY TO DAY PAMPHLETS NO. 14
§ Green paper wrappers printed in black.
45 pp. (5) $7\frac{1}{4}$ x $4\frac{3}{4}$.
Published November 1932; 1,500 copies printed.

305. **Quennell, Peter** *A Letter to Mrs. Virginia Woolf* Published by Leonard & Virginia Woolf at The Hogarth Press, 52 Tavistock Square, London, W.C.1 1932
THE HOGARTH LETTERS NO. 12
§ Cream paper wrappers printed in black and turquoise.
24 pp. (5) $7\frac{3}{8}$ x $4\frac{3}{4}$.
Published October 1932; 1,500 copies printed.

306. **Roberts, Michael** *New Signatures Poems by Several Hands* Collected by Michael Roberts. Published by Leonard & Virginia Woolf at The Hogarth Press, 52 Tavistock Square, London, W.C.1 1932
HOGARTH LIVING POETS, FIRST SERIES, NO. 24
§ Blue paper boards printed in gilt.
103 pp. (3) $7\frac{1}{2}$ x 5.
Published February 1932; 600 copies printed.
NOTE: I've seen a copy of the second impression that had a yellow paper wrap-around band printed *New Poems and Satires by* and listing the names of all the contributors.

307. **Sackville-West, V.** *Family History* Published by Leonard and Virginia Woolf at The Hogarth Press, Tavistock Square, London 1932
§ Orange cloth printed in gilt. White dust wrapper printed in grey and buff.
352 pp. (2) $7\frac{3}{8}$ x $4\frac{7}{8}$.
Published October 1932; 12,170 copies printed.

308. **Sadler, Sir Michael** *Modern Art and Revolution* Published by Leonard and Virginia Woolf at The Hogarth Press, 52 Tavistock Square London W.C. 1932
DAY TO DAY PAMPHLETS NO. 13
§ Green paper wrappers printed in black.
32 pp. (5) $7\frac{1}{4}$ x $4\frac{3}{4}$.
Published October 1932; 1,500 copies printed.

309. **Strachey, Julia** *Cheerful Weather for the Wedding* Published by Leonard and Virginia Woolf at The Hogarth Press, Tavistock Square, London 1932
§ Pale mauve paper boards with an over-all floral design; grey cloth spine printed in gilt. White dust wrapper printed in rose and blue.
119 pp. (2) $7\frac{1}{2}$ x $4\frac{3}{4}$.
Published September 1932; 1,212 copies printed.

310. **Strong, L. A. G.** *A Letter to W. B. Yeats* Published by Leonard & Virginia Woolf at The Hogarth Press, 52 Tavistock Square, London, W.C.1 1932
THE HOGARTH LETTERS NO. 6
§ Cream paper wrappers printed in blue and black.
31 pp. (5) $7\frac{3}{8}$ x $4\frac{3}{4}$.
Published January 1932; 2,000 copies printed.

311. **Trevelyan, R. C.** *Rimeless Numbers* Published by Leonard & Virginia Woolf at The Hogarth Press, 52 Tavistock Square, London, W.C.1 1932
§ Brown marbled paper boards; cream labels printed in black.
80 pp. (3) $8\frac{5}{8}$ x $5\frac{1}{2}$.
Published May 1932; 400 copies printed.

312. **Walpole, Hugh** *A Letter to a Modern Novelist* Published by Leonard & Virginia Woolf at The Hogarth Press, 52 Tavistock Square, London, W.C.1 1932
THE HOGARTH LETTERS NO. 9
§ Cream paper wrappers printed in black and purple.
29 pp. (5) $7\frac{3}{8}$ x $4\frac{3}{4}$.
Published July 1932; 2,500 copies printed.

313. **Wellesley, Dorothy** *Jupiter and the Nun* Printed & published by Leonard & Virginia Woolf at The Hogarth Press, London, 1932
§ Pale blue marbled paper boards printed in dark blue.
Unpaginated (1) $8\frac{3}{4}$ x $6\frac{3}{4}$.
Published May 1932; limited to 250 numbered and signed copies.
NOTE: The last book to be hand printed by the Woolfs.

314. **Woolf, Virginia** *A Letter to a Young Poet* Published by Leonard & Virginia Woolf at The Hogarth Press, 52 Tavistock Square, London, W.C.1 1932
THE HOGARTH LETTERS NO. 8
§ Cream paper wrappers printed in black and green.
28 pp. (5) $7\frac{3}{8}$ x $4\frac{3}{4}$.
Published July 1932; 6,000 copies printed.

315. **Woolf, Virginia** *The Common Reader Second Series* Published by Leonard & Virginia Woolf at The Hogarth Press, 52 Tavistock Square London, W.C. 1932
§ Bright green cloth printed in gilt. White dust wrapper printed in vermilion and azure.
270 pp. (2) $8\frac{1}{2}$ x $5\frac{5}{8}$.
Published October 1932; 3,200 copies printed.

1 9 3 3

316. **Bosanquet, Theodora** *Paul Valéry* Published by Leonard & Virginia Woolf at The Hogarth Press, 52 Tavistock Square, London, W.C. 1933
§ Cream paper boards printed in orange; orange cloth spine printed in black. Clear tissue dust wrapper printed in black.
136 pp. (5) $6\frac{1}{4}$ x 4.
Published February 1933; 1,000 copies printed.

317. **Bunin, Ivan**   *The Well of Days*   Translated from the Russian by Gleb Struve and Hamish Miles.   Published by Leonard and Virginia Woolf at The Hogarth Press, 52 Tavistock Square, London, W.C. 1933
§ Blue cloth printed in gilt. Dust wrapper not seen.
351 pp. (17) $7\frac{1}{2}$ x $4\frac{5}{8}$.
Published March 1933; 1,200 copies printed.

318A. **Day Lewis, C.**   *The Magnetic Mountain*   Published by Leonard & Virginia Woolf at The Hogarth Press, 52 Tavistock Square, London, W.C.1 1933
HOGARTH LIVING POETS, SECOND SERIES, NO. 1
§ Rose-brown cloth printed in gilt.
55 pp. (5) $7\frac{1}{2}$ x 5.
Published March 1933; limited to 100 numbered and signed copies.
NOTE: First (limited) edition.

318B. **Day Lewis, C.**   *The Magnetic Mountain*   Published by Leonard & Virginia Woolf at The Hogarth Press, 52 Tavistock Square, London, W.C.1 1933
HOGARTH LIVING POETS, SECOND SERIES, NO. 1
§ Grey paper boards printed in red.
55 pp. (5) $7\frac{1}{2}$ x 5.
Published March 1933; number of copies not known.
NOTE: First (trade) edition.

319. **Freud, Sigmund** *New Introductory Lectures on Psycho-Analysis* Edited by Ernest Jones.   Authorized Translation by W. J. H. Sprott.   Published by Leonard and Virginia Woolf at The Hogarth Press, 52 Tavistock Square, London, and The Institute of Psycho-Analysis 1933
THE INTERNATIONAL PSYCHO-ANALYTICAL LIBRARY NO. 24
§ Green cloth printed in gilt. Dust wrapper not seen.
240 pp. (2) $8\frac{3}{4}$ x $5\frac{1}{2}$.
Published November 1933; 2,040 copies printed.

320. **Greaves, H. R. G.** *The Spanish Constitution* Published by Leonard and Virginia Woolf at The Hogarth Press, 52 Tavistock Square London W.C. 1933
DAY TO DAY PAMPHLETS NO. 15
§ Yellow paper wrappers printed in black.
47 pp. (5) $7\frac{1}{4}$ x $4\frac{3}{4}$.
Published March 1933; number of copies not known.

321. *The Hogarth Letters* Published by Leonard & Virginia Woolf at The Hogarth Press, 52 Tavistock Square, London, W.C.1 1933
§ Buff paper boards printed in black and brown; brown cloth spine printed in black.
Separate pagination (5) $7\frac{1}{4}$ × $4\frac{3}{4}$.
Published February 1933; 500 copies issued.
NOTE: 500 copies of each volume in The Hogarth Letters series (with the exception of No. 7, Rebecca West's *A Letter to a Grandfather*) were bound together and issued in this collected volume with a new title page. Miss West's book wasn't published until March 1933.

322. **James, C. L. R.** *The Case for West-Indian Self Government* Published by Leonard and Virginia Woolf at The Hogarth Press, 52 Tavistock Square London W.C. 1933
DAY TO DAY PAMPHLETS NO. 16
§ Red paper wrappers printed in black.
32 pp. (5) $7\frac{1}{4}$ × $4\frac{3}{4}$.
Published April 1933; 1,200 copies printed.

323. **Leon, Derrick** *Livingstones* *A Novel of Contemporary Life* Published by Leonard and Virginia Woolf at The Hogarth Press, Tavistock Square, London 1933
§ Grey cloth printed in purple. White dust wrapper printed in grey and yellow.
653 pp. (2) $8\frac{3}{4}$ × $5\frac{1}{2}$.
Published February 1933; 1,512 copies printed.

324. **Madách, Imre** *The Tragedy of Man* Translated from the Hungarian by C. P. Sanger. Published by Leonard & Virginia Woolf at The Hogarth Press, 52 Tavistock Square, London, W.C.1 1933
§ Blue-grey cloth printed in black. Dust wrapper not seen.
155 pp. (5) $8\frac{5}{8}$ × $5\frac{1}{2}$.
Published October 1933; number of copies not known.

325. **Miller, Margaret** and **Douglas Campbell** *Financial Democracy* Published by Leonard and Virginia Woolf at The Hogarth Press, 52 Tavistock Square London W.C. 1933
§ Olive cloth printed in dark brown. Cream dust wrapper printed in green.
132 pp. (5) $7\frac{1}{2}$ × $4\frac{3}{4}$.
Published October 1933; 1,000 copies printed.

326. **Mussolini, Benito** *The Political and Social Doctrine of Fascism*
An authorized translation by Jane Soames. Published by
Leonard and Virginia Woolf at The Hogarth Press, 52
Tavistock Square London W.C. 1933
DAY TO DAY PAMPHLETS NO. 18
§ Pink paper wrappers printed in black.
26 pp. (5) $7\frac{1}{4}$ x $4\frac{3}{4}$.
Published October 1933; 1,500 copies printed.

327. **Olivier, Lord** *The Myth of Governor Eyre* Published by
Leonard & Virginia Woolf at The Hogarth Press, 52
Tavistock Square, London, W.C.1 1933
§ Salmon cloth printed in cream. Dust wrapper not seen.
348 pp. (5) $8\frac{1}{2}$ x 5.
Published October 1933; number of copies not known.

328. **Panikkar, K. M.** *Caste and Democracy* Published by
Leonard and Virginia Woolf at The Hogarth Press, 52
Tavistock Square London W.C. 1933
DAY TO DAY PAMPHLETS NO. 17
§ Violet paper wrappers printed in black.
39 pp. (5) $7\frac{1}{4}$ x $4\frac{3}{4}$.
Published October 1933; number of copies not known.

329. **Prophett, A.** *The Twilight Age, a Fragment of a Life* Published by Leonard and Virginia Woolf at The Hogarth
Press, Tavistock Square, London 1933
§ Grey cloth printed in blue. White dust wrapper printed
in black.
307 pp. (2) $7\frac{1}{2}$ x 5.
Published February 1933; 1,012 copies printed.

330. **Roberts, Michael, Editor** *New Country   Prose and Poetry
by the authors of* New Signatures. Published by Leonard
and Virginia Woolf at The Hogarth Press, 52 Tavistock
Square London W.C. 1933
§ Green cloth printed in gilt. Cream dust wrapper
printed in green.
256 pp. (5) $8\frac{3}{4}$ x $5\frac{1}{2}$.
Published March 1933; 1,200 copies printed.

331A. Sackville-West, V. *Collected Poems* Volume One Published by Leonard and Virginia Woolf at The Hogarth Press, Tavistock Square, London 1933
§ Brown cloth; white parchment spine printed in gilt. White dust wrapper printed in black.
325 pp. (2) $8\frac{3}{4}$ x $5\frac{3}{4}$.
Published November 1933; limited to 150 numbered and signed copies.
NOTE: First (limited) edition.
Volume Two was never published.

331B. Sackville-West, V. *Collected Poems* Volume One Published by Leonard and Virginia Woolf at The Hogarth Press, Tavistock Square, London 1933
§ Orange cloth printed in gilt. Cream dust wrapper printed in black.
325 pp. (2) $8\frac{3}{4}$ x $5\frac{1}{2}$.
Published November 1933; 3,045 copies printed.
NOTE: First (trade) edition.
Volume Two was never published.

332. Spaull, Hebe *How the World is Governed* *A Study in World Civics* Published by Leonard and Virginia Woolf at The Hogarth Press, 52 Tavistock Square, London, W.C.1 1933
§ Light brown paper-backed cloth wrappers printed in black.
72 pp. (5) 7 x $4\frac{1}{2}$.
Published February 1933; 2,500 copies printed.

333. West, Rebecca *A Letter to a Grandfather* Published by Leonard & Virginia Woolf at The Hogarth Press, 52 Tavistock Square, London, W.C.1 1933
THE HOGARTH LETTERS NO. 7
§ Cream paper wrappers printed in black and blue.
44 pp. (5) $7\frac{3}{8}$ x 5.
Published March 1933; 2,500 copies printed.
NOTE: The last volume to be published in this series, despite the low number, and the only one to be bound in overlapping wrappers.

334. Woolf, Virginia *Flush* *A Biography* Published by Leonard and Virginia Woolf at The Hogarth Press, 52 Tavistock Square, London, W.C. 1933

§ Buff cloth printed in gilt. Cream dust wrapper printed in brown.

163 pp. (2) $8\frac{1}{2}$ x $5\frac{3}{8}$.

Published October 1933; 12,680 copies printed.

NOTE: Called "Large Paper Edition" on the dust wrapper.

335. *The Worker's Point of View A Symposium* With a Preface by C. T. Cramp. Published by Leonard & Virginia Woolf at The Hogarth Press, 52 Tavistock Square, London, W.C.1 1933

§ Orange cloth printed in black. Cream dust wrapper printed in blue.

160 pp. (5) $7\frac{1}{2}$ x $4\frac{3}{4}$.

Published October 1933; 1,200 copies printed.

1 9 3 4

336. **Ballinger, W. G.** *Race and Economics in South Africa* Published by Leonard and Virginia Woolf at The Hogarth Press, 52 Tavistock Square, London, W.C. 1934

DAY TO DAY PAMPHLETS NO. 21

§ Orange paper wrappers printed in black.

67 pp. (5) $7\frac{1}{4}$ x $4\frac{3}{4}$.

Published May 1934; 2,000 copies printed.

NOTE: Also issued in orange cloth printed in black; orange dust wrapper printed in black.

337. **Blunden, Edmund** *Charles Lamb His Life Recorded by his Contemporaries* Compiled by Edmund Blunden. London, 1934 Published by Leonard and Virginia Woolf at The Hogarth Press, 52 Tavistock Square, W.C.1

BIOGRAPHIES THROUGH THE EYES OF CONTEMPORARIES SERIES NO. 1

§ Orange cloth printed in white. Dust wrapper not seen.

256 pp. (5) $8\frac{3}{4}$ x $5\frac{1}{2}$.

Published March 1934; 1,500 copies printed.

338. **Butler, Constance** *Illyria, Lady* Published by Leonard and Virginia Woolf at The Hogarth Press, Tavistock Square, London 1934

§ Yellow cloth printed in gilt. Blue dust wrapper printed in red.

228 pp. (2) $7\frac{3}{8}$ x $4\frac{3}{4}$.

Published October 1934; number of copies not known.

339. **Gorky, Maxim** *Reminiscences of Tolstoy Chekhov and Andreev* Authorized translation from the Russian by Katherine Mansfield, S. S. Koteliansky and Leonard Woolf. Published by Leonard and Virginia Woolf at The Hogarth Press, 52 Tavistock Square, London, W.C. 1934
§ Blue cloth printed in gilt. Grey dust wrapper printed in blue.
191 pp. (5) $8\frac{1}{2}$ x $5\frac{3}{8}$.
Published October 1934; 1,250 copies printed.

340. **Graham, John L.** *Good Merchant* Published by Leonard and Virginia Woolf at The Hogarth Press, 52 Tavistock Square, London, W.C.1 1934
§ Orange cloth printed in gilt. White dust wrapper printed in black and yellow.
288 pp. (5) $7\frac{1}{2}$ x 5.
Published September 1934; number of copies not known.

341. **Kitchin, C. H. B.** *Crime at Christmas* Published by Leonard and Virginia Woolf at The Hogarth Press, 52 Tavistock Square, London, W.C.1 1934
§ Red cloth printed in black. Dust wrapper not seen.
285 pp. (5) $7\frac{1}{2}$ x $4\frac{3}{4}$.
Published October 1934; number of copies not known.

342A. **Lehmann, John** *The Noise of History* Published by Leonard & Virginia Woolf at The Hogarth Press, 52 Tavistock Square, London, W.C.1 1934
HOGARTH LIVING POETS, SECOND SERIES, NO. 2
§ Pink-buff cloth printed in gilt. Pink-buff dust wrapper printed in black.
62 pp. (5) $7\frac{1}{2}$ x 5.
Published September 1934; limited to 75 numbered and signed copies.
NOTE: First (limited) edition. Printed on heavier paper than the trade edition and a leaf with a limitation statement is substituted for the advertisement leaf.

342B. **Lehmann, John** *The Noise of History* Published by Leonard & Virginia Woolf at The Hogarth Press, 52 Tavistock Square, London, W.C.1 1934
HOGARTH LIVING POETS, SECOND SERIES, NO. 2

§ Pale blue-green paper boards printed in red.
62 pp. (5) $7\frac{1}{2}$ x 5.
Published September 1934; 550 copies printed.
NOTE: First (trade) edition.

343. **Mockerie, Parmenas Githendu** *An African Speaks for his People* With a Foreword by Professor Julian Huxley. Published by Leonard and Virginia Woolf at The Hogarth Press, 52 Tavistock Square, London, W.C. 1934
§ Light brown cloth printed in black. Buff dust wrapper printed in red.
95 pp. (5) $7\frac{3}{8}$ x $4\frac{7}{8}$.
Published February 1934; **1,150 copies printed.**

344. **Pekin, L. B.** *Progressive Schools Their Principles and Practice* Published by Leonard and Virginia Woolf at The Hogarth Press, 52 Tavistock Square, London, W.C. 1934
§ Green cloth printed in white.   Buff dust wrapper printed in green.
197 pp. (3) $7\frac{1}{4}$ x $4\frac{3}{8}$.
Published February 1934; **1,270 copies printed.**
NOTE: L. B. Pekin is a pseudonym for Reginald Snell.

345. **Petroff, Peter & Irma** *The Secret of Hitler's Victory* Published by Leonard and Virginia Woolf at The Hogarth Press, 52 Tavistock Square, London, W.C. 1934
§ Red-brown cloth printed in black. Brown dust wrapper printed in dark brown.
128 pp. (5) $7\frac{3}{8}$ x $4\frac{3}{4}$.
Published August 1934; number of copies not known.

346. **Postgate, Raymond** *How to Make a Revolution* Published by Leonard and Virginia Woolf at The Hogarth Press, 52 Tavistock Square, London, W.C. 1934
§ Red cloth printed in black. Dust wrapper not seen.
199 pp. (5) $7\frac{3}{8}$ x $4\frac{7}{8}$.
Published October 1934; **1,920 copies printed.**

347. **Ratcliffe, S. K.** *The Roots of Violence* Published by Leonard and Virginia Woolf at The Hogarth Press, 52 Tavistock Square, London, W.C. 1934

THE MERTTENS LECTURE 1934

DAY TO DAY PAMPHLETS NO. 22

§ Yellow paper wrappers printed in black (see note).
60 pp. (5) $7\frac{1}{4}$ x $4\frac{3}{4}$.
Published July 1934; 1,500 copies printed.
NOTE: Also issued in grey cloth printed in black; yellow dust wrapper printed in black.

348. **Rilke, Rainer Maria** *Poems* Translated from the German by J. B. Leishman. London 1934 Published by Leonard & Virginia Woolf at The Hogarth Press, Tavistock Square

§ Grey cloth printed in black. Yellow dust wrapper printed in black.
51 pp. (9) $8\frac{1}{4}$ x $5\frac{1}{4}$.
Published February 1934; 1,020 copies printed.

349. **Roheim, Geza** *The Riddle of the Sphinx or Human Origins* Authorized translation from the German by R. Money-Kyrle. With a Preface by Ernest Jones. Published by Leonard and Virginia Woolf at The Hogarth Press, 52 Tavistock Square, London, and The Institute of Psycho-Analysis 1934

THE INTERNATIONAL PSYCHO-ANALYTICAL LIBRARY NO. 25

§ Green cloth printed in gilt. Dust wrapper not seen.
302 pp. (2) $8\frac{5}{8}$ x $5\frac{1}{2}$.
Published October 1934; 770 copies printed.

350. **Rowse, A. L.** *The Question of the House of Lords* Published by Leonard and Virginia Woolf at The Hogarth Press, 52 Tavistock Square, London, W.C. 1934

DAY TO DAY PAMPHLETS NO. 19

§ Blue paper wrappers printed in black.
64 pp. (5) $7\frac{1}{4}$ x $4\frac{3}{4}$.
Published October 1934; 2,000 copies printed.

351. **Sackville-West, V.** *The dark island* Published by Leonard & Virginia Woolf The Hogarth Press, Tavistock Square 1934
§ Light green cloth printed in dark green. White dust wrapper printed in black.
317 pp. (2) $7\frac{1}{2}$ x $4\frac{3}{4}$.
Published October 1934; 10,590 copies printed.

352. **Sutherland, James** *The Medium of Poetry* Published by Leonard & Virginia Woolf at The Hogarth Press, 52 Tavistock Square, London, W.C.1 1934
HOGARTH LECTURES ON LITERATURE, SECOND SERIES, NO. 1
§ Brown cloth printed in dark brown. Buff dust wrapper printed in dark brown.
168 pp. (5) $7\frac{3}{8}$ x $4\frac{3}{4}$.
Published February 1934; 1,200 copies printed.

353. **Van der Post, Laurens** *In a Province* London, 1934 Published by Leonard and Virginia Woolf at The Hogarth Press, 52 Tavistock Square, W.C.1
§ Green cloth printed in dark blue. Buff dust wrapper printed in red-brown.
350 pp. (5) $7\frac{1}{2}$ x $4\frac{7}{8}$.
Published February 1934; 1,250 copies printed.

354. **Watson, W. F.** *The Worker and Wage Incentives: The Bedaux and Other Systems* Published by Leonard and Virginia Woolf at The Hogarth Press, 52 Tavistock Square, London, W.C. 1934
DAY TO DAY PAMPHLETS NO. 20
§ Red paper wrappers printed in black.
46 pp. (5) $7\frac{1}{4}$ x $4\frac{3}{4}$.
Published May 1934; 1,500 copies printed.
NOTE: Also issued in cloth and dust wrapper but I haven't seen a copy.

355. **Woolf, Virginia** *Walter Sickert A Conversation* Published by Leonard and Virginia Woolf at The Hogarth Press, 52 Tavistock Square, London, W.C.1 1934
§ Pale blue paper wrappers printed in black.
28 pp. (5) $7\frac{1}{4}$ x $4\frac{7}{8}$.
Published October 1934; 3,800 copies printed.

356. **Z., Y.** *From Moscow to Samarkand* By Y. Z. London 1934
Published by Leonard and Virginia Woolf at The Hogarth Press, 52 Tavistock Square, W.C.1
§ Red cloth printed in white. Buff dust wrapper printed in black.
134 pp. (5) $8\frac{1}{2}$ x $5\frac{3}{8}$.
Published February 1934; 1,200 copies printed.
NOTE: Y. Z. is a pseudonym for Freda Utley.

1 9 3 5

357. **Bailey, S. H.** *Mr. Roosevelt's Experiments* Published by Leonard and Virginia Woolf at The Hogarth Press, 52 Tavistock Square, London, W.C. 1935

DAY TO DAY PAMPHLETS NO. 24

§ Blue paper wrappers printed in black.
48 pp. (5) $7\frac{1}{4}$ x $4\frac{3}{4}$.
Published February 1935; 1,500 copies printed.

358. **Birkinshaw, Mary** *The Successful Teacher An Occupational Analysis based on an enquiry conducted among women teachers in secondary schools* Published by Leonard and Virginia Woolf at The Hogarth Press, 52 Tavistock Square, London, W.C. 1935
§ Orange cloth printed in black. Orange dust wrapper printed in black.
128 pp. (5) $7\frac{1}{2}$ x $4\frac{3}{4}$.
Published October 1935; 1,500 copies printed.

359. **Brewster, Ralph** *The 6,000 Beards of Athos* With a Preface by Ethel Smyth. Published by Leonard and Virginia Woolf at The Hogarth Press, 52 Tavistock Square, London, W.C. 1935
§ Green cloth printed in gilt. Pale blue dust wrapper printed in black.
219 pp. plus plates (5) $8\frac{3}{8}$ x $6\frac{1}{2}$.
Published October 1935; number of copies not known.

360. **Buchan, Susan** *Funeral March of a Marionette Charlotte of Albany* Published by Leonard and Virginia Woolf at The Hogarth Press, 52 Tavistock Square, London, W.C.1 1935
§ Black cloth printed in gilt. Blue dust wrapper printed in red.
96 pp. (5) $7\frac{1}{2}$ x $4\frac{3}{4}$.
Published October 1935; 1,500 copies printed.

361. **Bunin, Ivan**   *Grammar of Love*   Translated by John Cournos. Published by Leonard and Virginia Woolf at The Hogarth Press, 52 Tavistock Square, London, W.C.1 1935

§ Grey cloth printed in black.   Orange dust wrapper printed in red.

221 pp. (6) $7\frac{1}{2}$ x $4\frac{3}{4}$.

Published March 1935; number of copies not known.

362. **Calder-Marshall, Arthur**   *Challenge to Schools   A pamphlet on Public School Education*   Published by Leonard and Virginia Woolf at The Hogarth Press, 52 Tavistock Square, London, W.C.   1935

DAY TO DAY PAMPHLETS NO. 27

§ Buff paper wrappers printed in green.

43 pp. (5) $7\frac{1}{4}$ x $4\frac{3}{4}$.

Published September 1935; 1,200 copies printed.

363. **Day Lewis, C.**   *Collected Poems 1929-1933*   Published by Leonard and Virginia Woolf at The Hogarth Press   Tavistock Square   London   1935

§ Lime green cloth printed in dark green.   Gold dust wrapper printed in black.

156 pp. (6) $8\frac{1}{2}$ x $5\frac{1}{2}$.

Published March 1935; 620 copies printed.

364. **Day Lewis, C.**   *A Time to Dance and Other Poems*   Published by Leonard & Virginia Woolf at The Hogarth Press, 52 Tavistock Square, London, W.C.1   1935

§ Red cloth printed in gilt.   Cream dust wrapper printed in red.

64 pp. (5) $8\frac{5}{8}$ x $5\frac{5}{8}$.

Published March 1935; 750 copies printed.

365. **Day Lewis, C.**   *Revolution in Writing*   Published by Leonard and Virginia Woolf at The Hogarth Press, 52 Tavistock Square, London, W.C.   1935

DAY TO DAY PAMPHLETS NO. 29

§ Pink paper wrappers printed in blue.

44 pp. (5) $7\frac{1}{4}$ x $4\frac{3}{4}$.

Published October 1935; 1,500 copies printed.

366. **Delafield, E. M.** *The Brontës Their Lives Recorded by their Contemporaries* Compiled with an Introduction by E. M. Delafield. London, 1935 Published by Leonard and Virginia Woolf at The Hogarth Press, 52 Tavistock Square, W.C.1

BIOGRAPHIES THROUGH THE EYES OF CONTEMPORARIES SERIES NO. 2

§ Red cloth printed in white. Cream dust wrapper printed in black.

274 pp. (5) $8\frac{3}{4}$ x $5\frac{1}{2}$.

Published May 1935; 2,000 copies printed.

NOTE: E. M. Delafield is a pseudonym for Edmée Elizabeth Monica De La Pasture, *later* Dashwood.

367. **Freud, Sigmund** *An Autobiographical Study* Authorized Translation by James Strachey. Published by Leonard and Virginia Woolf at The Hogarth Press, 52 Tavistock Square, London, and The Institute of Psycho-Analysis 1935

THE INTERNATIONAL PSYCHO-ANALYTICAL LIBRARY NO. 26

§ Green cloth printed in gilt. Dust wrapper not seen.

137 pp. (2) $8\frac{1}{2}$ x $5\frac{1}{2}$.

Published December 1935; 1,768 copies printed.

368. **Gooch, G. P.** *Politics and Morals* Published by Leonard and Virginia Woolf at The Hogarth Press, 52 Tavistock Square, London, W.C. 1935

THE MERTTENS LECTURE 1935

DAY TO DAY PAMPHLETS NO. 30

§ Yellow paper wrappers printed in black.

51 pp. (5) $7\frac{1}{4}$ x $4\frac{3}{4}$.

Published October 1935; number of copies not known.

369. **Isherwood, Christopher** *Mr. Norris changes Trains* Published by Leonard and Virginia Woolf at The Hogarth Press, 52 Tavistock Square, London, W.C.1 1935

§ Green cloth printed in black. Yellow dust wrapper printed in dark brown.

280 pp. (5) $7\frac{3}{8}$ x $4\frac{7}{8}$.

Published March 1935; 1,730 copies printed.

370. **Laski, Harold J.** *Law and Justice in Soviet Russia* Published by Leonard and Virginia Woolf at The Hogarth Press, 52 Tavistock Square, London, W.C. 1935
DAY TO DAY PAMPHLETS NO. 23
§ Dark red paper wrappers printed in black.
44 pp. (5) $7\frac{1}{4}$ x $4\frac{3}{4}$.
Published February 1935; 3,000 copies printed.

371. **Lester, W. R.** *Poverty and Plenty: The True National Dividend* Published by The Hogarth Press, 52 Tavistock Square, London, W.C.1 for the Henry George Foundation of Great Britian 1935
DAY TO DAY PAMPHLETS NO. 26
§ Green paper wrappers printed in black.
21 pp. (5) $7\frac{1}{4}$ x $4\frac{3}{4}$.
Published June 1935; number of copies not known.

372. **Mauron, Charles** *Aesthetics and Psychology* Translated from the French by Roger Fry and Katherine John. Published by Leonard and Virginia Woolf at The Hogarth Press, 52 Tavistock Square, London, W.C. 1935
§ Orange cloth printed in black. Grey dust wrapper printed in black.
110 pp. (5) $7\frac{3}{8}$ x $4\frac{3}{4}$.
Published May 1935; 1,000 copies printed.

373. **Origo, Iris** *Allegra* Published by Leonard and Virginia Woolf at The Hogarth Press, 52 Tavistock Square, London, W.C. 1935
§ Yellow cloth printed in brown. Green dust wrapper printed in black.
119 pp. (2) $8\frac{5}{8}$ x $5\frac{1}{2}$.
Published October 1935; 1,268 copies printed.

374. **Postgate, Raymond** *What to do with the B.B.C.* Published by Leonard and Virginia Woolf at The Hogarth Press, 52 Tavistock Square, London, W.C. 1935
DAY TO DAY PAMPHLETS NO. 28
§ Green paper wrappers printed in black.
68 pp. (5) $7\frac{1}{4}$ x $4\frac{3}{4}$.
Published September 1935; 1,500 copies printed.

375. **Rilke, Rainer Maria** *Requiem and Other Poems* Translated from the German with an Introduction by J. B. Leishman. London 1935 Published by Leonard & Virginia Woolf at The Hogarth Press, Tavistock Square
§ Brown cloth printed in gilt. Green dust wrapper printed in black.
147 pp. (9) $8\frac{5}{8}$ x $5\frac{1}{2}$.
Published May 1935; 1,075 copies printed.

376. **Sharp, Thomas** *A Derelict Area A Study of the South-West Durham Coalfield* With an Introduction by Hugh Dalton. Published by Leonard and Virginia Woolf at The Hogarth Press, 52 Tavistock Square, London, W.C. 1935
DAY TO DAY PAMPHLETS NO. 25
§ Yellow paper wrappers printed in black.
49 pp. (5) $7\frac{1}{4}$ x $4\frac{3}{4}$.
Published February 1935; number of copies not known.

377. **Trevelyan, R. C.** *Beelzebub and Other Poems* Published by Leonard & Virginia Woolf at The Hogarth Press, 52 Tavistock Square, London, W.C.1 1935
HOGARTH LIVING POETS, SECOND SERIES, NO. 3
§ Pale green paper boards printed in red.
59 pp. (5) $7\frac{1}{2}$ x 5.
Published October 1935; **400 copies printed.**

378. **Verinder, Frederick** *Land and Freedom* Published by Leonard and Virginia Woolf at The Hogarth Press 52, Tavistock Square, London, W.C.5 1935
§ Green cloth printed in gilt. Dust wrapper not seen.
199 pp. (25) $7\frac{1}{2}$ x $4\frac{3}{4}$.
Published September 1935; 500 copies printed.

379. **Whyte, Anna D.** *Change your Sky* Published by Leonard and Virginia Woolf at The Hogarth Press, 52 Tavistock Square, London, W.C.1 1935
§ Blue cloth printed in gilt. Cream dust wrapper printed in blue.
302 pp. (5) $7\frac{3}{4}$ x $4\frac{7}{8}$.
Published March 1935; 1,200 copies printed.

380. **Woolf, Leonard** *Quack, Quack!* Published by Leonard and Virginia Woolf at the Hogarth Press, 52 Tavistock Square, London, W.C. 1935
§ Green cloth printed in gilt. White dust wrapper printed in blue, black, and red.
201 pp. (2) $7\frac{3}{8}$ x $4\frac{3}{4}$.
Published May 1935; number of copies not known.

1 9 3 6

381. **Barnes, Leonard** *The Future of Colonies* Published by Leonard and Virginia Woolf at The Hogarth Press, 52 Tavistock Square, London, W.C. 1936
DAY TO DAY PAMPHLETS NO. 32
§ Blue paper wrappers printed in dark blue.
46 pp. (5) $7\frac{1}{4}$ x $4\frac{3}{4}$.
Published March 1936; 2,000 copies printed.

382. **Bell, Julian** *Work for the Winter and other poems* Published by Leonard & Virginia Woolf at The Hogarth Press, 52 Tavistock Square, London, W.C.1 1936
HOGARTH LIVING POETS, SECOND SERIES, NO. 4
§ Grey paper boards printed in black.
68 pp. (5) $7\frac{1}{2}$ x 5.
Published March 1936; **750 copies printed.**

383A. **Day Lewis, C.** *Noah and the Waters* Published by Leonard & Virginia Woolf at The Hogarth Press, 52 Tavistock Square, London, W.C.1 1936
§ Fawn cloth printed in gilt. Light blue-green dust wrapper printed in green.
59 pp. (5) $8\frac{1}{2}$ x $5\frac{1}{2}$.
Published February 1936; limited to 100 numbered and signed copies.
NOTE: First (limited) edition.

383B. **Day Lewis, C.** *Noah and the Waters* Published by Leonard & Virginia Woolf at The Hogarth Press, 52 Tavistock Square, London, W.C.1 1936
§ Yellow cloth printed in gilt. Light buff dust wrapper printed in red.
59 pp. (5) $8\frac{1}{2}$ x $5\frac{1}{2}$.
Published February 1936; 2,000 copies printed.
NOTE: First (trade) edition.

384. Douglas, F. C. R. *Land-Value Rating Theory and Practice*
Published by Leonard and Virginia Woolf at The Hogarth Press, 52 Tavistock Square, London, W.C.1 1936
§ Blue cloth printed in gilt. Buff dust wrapper printed in blue.
76 pp. (25) $7\frac{1}{2}$ x 5.
Published May 1936; number of copies not known.

385. Faulkner, Fritz *Windless Sky* Published by Leonard and Virginia Woolf at The Hogarth Press, 52 Tavistock Square, London, W.C. 1936
§ Light blue cloth printed in gilt. Blue dust wrapper printed in dark blue.
295 pp. (5) $7\frac{3}{8}$ x $4\frac{1}{2}$.
Published October 1936; **1,080 copies printed.**

386. Freud, Sigmund *Inhibitions, Symptoms and Anxiety* Authorized translation by Alix Strachey. Published by Leonard and Virginia Woolf at The Hogarth Press, 52 Tavistock Square, London, and The Institute of Psycho-Analysis 1936
THE INTERNATIONAL PSYCHO-ANALYTICAL LIBRARY NO. 28
§ Green cloth printed in gilt. Green dust wrapper printed in black.
179 pp. (2) $8\frac{1}{2}$ x $5\frac{1}{2}$.
Published November 1936; **2,500 copies printed.**

387. Friends Anti-War Group *The Roots of War A Pamphlet on War and the Social Order* This pamphlet is written by eight members of the Friends Anti-War Group and the No More War Movement. Published by Leonard and Virginia Woolf at The Hogarth Press, 52 Tavistock Square, London, W.C. 1936
§ Green paper wrappers printed in black.
72 pp. (30) 7 x $4\frac{5}{8}$.
Published January 1936; number of copies not known.
NOTE: Second edition, but first Hogarth Press edition. The following appears on verso of title page "The first edition of this pamphlet was published jointly by the Friends Anti-War Group and the No More War Movement in May 1935, and was exhausted within six months of publication." "Second edition" appears on top cover and title page.

388. **Gordon, Mary** *Chase of the Wild Goose The story of Lady Eleanor Butler and Miss Sarah Ponsonby, known as the Ladies of Llangollen* Published by Leonard and Virginia Woolf at The Hogarth Press, 52 Tavistock Square, London, W.C.1 1936
§ Blue cloth printed in gilt. White dust wrapper printed in black and green.
279 pp. (5) $8\frac{5}{8} \times 5\frac{1}{2}$.
Published May 1936; 1,200 copies printed.

389. **Innes, Kathleen E.** *The League of Nations The complete story told for young people* Published by Leonard and Virginia Woolf at The Hogarth Press, 52 Tavistock Square, London, W.C. 1936
§ Red cloth printed in black. Dust wrapper not seen.
166 pp. (5) $7\frac{1}{4} \times 4\frac{3}{4}$.
Published May 1936; 2,500 copies printed.

390. **Millard, A. Douglas** *The Co-operative Movement To-day and To-morrow* Published by Leonard and Virginia Woolf at The Hogarth Press, 52 Tavistock Square, London, W.C. 1936
DAY TO DAY PAMPHLETS NO. 33
§ Brown paper wrappers printed in green.
61 pp. (31) $7\frac{1}{4} \times 4\frac{3}{4}$.
Published October 1936; 2,750 copies printed.

391. **Olyesha, Yuri** *Envy* Translated from the Russian by Anthony Wolfe. Published by Leonard and Virginia Woolf at The Hogarth Press, 52 Tavistock Square, London, W.C.1 1936
§ Red cloth printed in gilt. Dust wrapper not seen.
275 pp. (2) $7\frac{1}{4} \times 4\frac{3}{4}$.
Published October 1936; 1,778 copies printed.

392. **Reik, Theodor** *The Unknown Murderer* Translated from the German by Dr. Katherine Jones. Published by Leonard and Virginia Woolf at The Hogarth Press, 52 Tavistock Square, London, and The Institute of Psycho-Analysis 1936
THE INTERNATIONAL PSYCHO-ANALYTICAL LIBRARY NO. 27
§ Green cloth printed in gilt. Green dust wrapper printed in black.
260 pp. (5) $8\frac{3}{4} \times 5\frac{1}{2}$.
Published October 1936; 1,100 copies printed.

393. **Rilke, Rainer Maria** *Sonnets to Orpheus Written as a mon-ument for Wera Ouckama Knoop* The German Text, with an English Translation, Introduction & Notes by J. B. Leish-man.   London   Published by Leonard & Virginia Woolf at The Hogarth Press, Tavistock Square   1936
§ Light tan cloth printed in black. Orange dust wrapper printed in black.
188 pp. (9) $8\frac{1}{4}$ x $5\frac{1}{4}$.
Published October 1936; 1,020 copies printed.

394. **Salter, Sir Arthur** *Economic Policies and Peace* Published by Leonard and Virginia Woolf at The Hogarth Press, 52 Tavistock Square, London, W.C. 1936
THE MERTTENS LECTURE 1936
DAY TO DAY PAMPHLETS NO. 34
§ Orange paper wrappers printed in black.
38 pp. (5) $7\frac{1}{4}$ x $4\frac{3}{4}$.
Published December 1936; 2,235 copies printed.

395. **Securitas** *Adventures in Investing by "Securitas"* (*Financial Editor of* Time and Tide) Published by Leonard and Vir-ginia Woolf at The Hogarth Press, 52 Tavistock Square, London, W.C. 1936
§ Red cloth printed in gilt. Dust wrapper not seen.
208 pp. (5) 7 x $4\frac{1}{2}$.
Published June 1936; 2,500 copies printed.

396. **Stephen, Adrian** *The "Dreadnought" Hoax* Published by Leonard and Virginia Woolf at The Hogarth Press, 52 Tavistock Square, London, W.C. 1936
§ Buff paper boards printed in brown.
47 pp. (5) $7\frac{1}{2}$ x $4\frac{7}{8}$.
Published November 1936; 2,530 copies printed.

397. **Strachey, Ray, Editor** *Our Freedom and its Results by Five Women, Eleanor F. Rathbone, Erna Reiss, Ray Strachey, Allison Neilans, Mary Agnes Hamilton* Published by Leonard and Virginia Woolf at The Hogarth Press, 52 Tavistock Square, London, W.C.1 1936
§ Blue cloth printed in gilt. Cream dust wrapper printed in blue.
285 pp. (5) $8\frac{5}{8}$ x $5\frac{1}{2}$.
Published October 1936; 2,556 copies printed.

398. **Swinstead-Smith, K.** *The Marchesa and Other Stories*
Published by Leonard and Virginia Woolf at The Ho-
garth Press, 52 Tavistock Square, London, W.C.1   1936
§ Blue cloth printed in black. Mauve dust wrapper
printed in brown.
238 pp. (5) $7\frac{3}{8}$ x $4\frac{3}{4}$.
Published March 1936; 1,200 copies printed.
NOTE: K. Swinstead-Smith is a pseudonym for Kay Thomas.

399. **Tolstoy, Leo** *On Socialism*   Translated from the Russian by Ludvig Perno. Published by Leonard and Virginia
Woolf at The Hogarth Press, 52 Tavistock Square, London, W.C.   1936
§ Pink paper wrappers printed in black.
24 pp. (5) 7 x $4\frac{1}{2}$.
Published March 1936; 2,000 copies printed.

400. **Wells, H. G.** *The Idea of a World Encyclopaedia   A Lecture
Delivered at the Royal Institution, November 20th, 1936*   Pub-
lished by Leonard and Virginia Woolf at The Hogarth
Press, 52 Tavistock Square, London, W.C.   1936
DAY TO DAY PAMPHLETS NO. 35
§ Green paper wrappers printed in black.
32 pp. (5) $7\frac{1}{4}$ x $4\frac{3}{4}$.
Published November 1936; 2,200 copies printed.

401. **Whyte, Anna D.** *Lights Are Bright*   Published by Leonard and Virginia Woolf at The Hogarth Press, 52 Tavistock Square, London W.C.1   1936
§ Green cloth printed in gilt. Dust wrapper not seen.
320 pp. (5) 7 x $4\frac{1}{2}$.
Published October 1936; 1,219 copies printed.

402. **Willis, Irene Cooper** *The Authorship of Wuthering Heights*
Published by Leonard and Virginia Woolf at The Hogarth
Press, 52 Tavistock Square, London, W.C.1   1936
§ Grey cloth printed in black. Dust wrapper not seen.
94 pp. (5) $7\frac{3}{8}$ x $4\frac{7}{8}$.
Published March 1936; 1,200 copies printed.

403. **Woolf, Leonard** *The League and Abyssinia* Published by
Leonard and Virginia Woolf at The Hogarth Press, 52
Tavistock Square, London, W.C. 1936
DAY TO DAY PAMPHLETS NO. 31
§ Salmon paper wrappers printed in black.
35 pp. (5) $7\frac{1}{4}$ x $4\frac{3}{4}$.
Published March 1936; 2,200 copies printed.

1 9 3 7

404. **Allinson, Francesca** *A Childhood.* With wood engrav-
ings by Enid Marx. Published by Leonard & Virginia
Woolf at The Hogarth Press, 52 Tavistock Square, London, W.C.1 1937
§ Blue cloth printed in gilt. Cream dust wrapper printed
in blue and black.
187 pp. (5) $8\frac{5}{8}$ x $5\frac{3}{8}$.
Published October 1937; number of copies not known.

405. **(Amberley, Lord and Lady)** *The Amberley Papers The
Letters and Diaries of Lord and Lady Amberley* Edited by
Bertrand and Patricia Russell. Published by Leonard &
Virginia Woolf at The Hogarth Press, 52 Tavistock
Square, London, W.C.1 1937 2 volumes
§ Green cloth printed in gilt. Dust wrappers not seen.
552 pp. and 581 pp. (5) 9 x $5\frac{1}{2}$.
Published March 1937; number of copies not known.

406. **Delafield, E. M.** *Ladies and Gentlemen in Victorian Fiction*
Published by Leonard & Virginia Woolf at The Hogarth
Press, 52 Tavistock Square, London, W.C.1 1937
§ Blue cloth printed in gilt. Cream dust wrapper printed
in black.
294 pp. (5) $8\frac{5}{8}$ x $5\frac{1}{2}$.
Published June 1937; 1,500 copies printed.
NOTE: E. M. Delafield is a pseudonym for Edmée Elizabeth Monica
De La Pasture, *later* Dashwood.

407. **Fox, R. M.** *Smoky Crusade* Published by Leonard and
Virginia Woolf at The Hogarth Press, 52 Tavistock
Square, London, W.C. 1937
§ Red cloth printed in gilt. White dust wrapper print-
ed in black, red, and blue.
368 pp. (5) $8\frac{5}{8}$ x $5\frac{3}{8}$.
Published March 1937; 1,250 copies printed.

408. **Freud, Anna** *The Ego and the Mechanisms of Defence* Translated from the German by Cecil Baines. Published by Leonard and Virginia Woolf at The Hogarth Press, 52 Tavistock Square, London, and The Institute of Psycho-Analysis 1937
THE INTERNATIONAL PSYCHO-ANALYTICAL LIBRARY NO. 30
§ Green cloth printed in gilt. Dust wrapper not seen. 196 pp. (5) $8\frac{3}{4}$ x $5\frac{1}{2}$.
Published October 1937; 1,225 copies printed.

409. **Freud, Sigmund** *A General Selection from the Works of Sigmund Freud* Edited by John Rickman. Published by Leonard and Virginia Woolf at The Hogarth Press, 52 Tavistock Square, London, and The Institute of Psycho-Analysis 1937
PSYCHO-ANALYTICAL EPITOMES NO. 1
§ Blue cloth printed in gilt. Dust wrapper not seen. 329 pp. (5) $7\frac{1}{2}$ x 5.
Published November 1937; 3,045 copies printed.

410. **Harris, Dr. I.** *Diet and High Blood Pressure* Published by Leonard and Virginia Woolf at The Hogarth Press, 52 Tavistock Square, London, W.C.1 1937
§ Green cloth printed in gilt. Orange dust wrapper printed in black.
196 pp. (5) $8\frac{3}{4}$ x $5\frac{1}{2}$.
Published April 1937; 1,780 copies printed.

411. **Isherwood, Christopher** *Sally Bowles* Published by Leonard and Virginia Woolf at The Hogarth Press, 52 Tavistock Square, London, W.C.2 1937
§ Blue cloth printed in black. Peach dust wrapper printed in green.
150 pp. (5) $6\frac{5}{8}$ x 4.
Published November 1937; 2,040 copies printed.

412. **Klein, Melanie & Joan Riviere** *Love, Hate and Reparation* Published by Leonard and Virginia Woolf at The Hogarth Press, 52 Tavistock Square, London, and The Institute of Psycho-Analysis 1937
PSYCHO-ANALYTICAL EPITOMES NO. 2   (Cont'd)

§ Stiff white unprinted paper wrappers.　White dust wrapper printed in black.

119 pp. (5) $7\frac{1}{2}$ × $4\frac{7}{8}$.

Published November 1937; 1,624 copies printed.

NOTE: The only copy I've seen had "For Author's Distribution Only" printed on the dust wrapper.

413. **Lee, Christopher** *Poems* Published by Leonard & Virginia Woolf at The Hogarth Press, 52 Tavistock Square, London, W.C.1　1937

HOGARTH LIVING POETS, SECOND SERIES, NO. 5

§ Light blue paper boards printed in dark blue.

62 pp. (5) $7\frac{1}{2}$ × 5.

Published March 1937; 450 copies printed.

414. **Lowe, Adolf** *The Price of Liberty A German on Contemporary Britain* Published by Leonard and Virginia Woolf at The Hogarth Press, 52 Tavistock Square, London, W.C. 1937

DAY TO DAY PAMPHLETS NO. 36

§ Red paper wrappers printed in black.

44 pp. (5) $7\frac{1}{4}$ × $4\frac{3}{4}$.

Published March 1937; number of copies not known.

415. **Mitchison, Naomi** and **R.H.S. Crossman** *Socrates* Published by Leonard and Virginia Woolf at The Hogarth Press, 52 Tavistock Square, London, W.C. 1937

WORLD-MAKERS & WORLD-SHAKERS SERIES

§ Brown cloth printed in black. Yellow dust wrapper printed in green.

80 pp. (5) $7\frac{1}{4}$ × $4\frac{3}{4}$.

Published June 1937; 5,000 copies printed.

416. **Pekin, L. B.** *The Military Training of Youth An enquiry into the aims and effects of the O. T. C.* Published by Leonard and Virginia Woolf at The Hogarth Press, 52 Tavistock Square, London, W.C. 1937

DAY TO DAY PAMPHLETS NO. 37

§ Yellow paper wrappers printed in black.

53 pp. (5) $7\frac{1}{4}$ × $4\frac{3}{4}$.

Published May 1937; 1,500 copies printed.

NOTE: L. B. Pekin is a pseudonym for Reginald Snell.

417. **Pekin, L.B.** *Darwin* Published by Leonard and Virginia Woolf at The Hogarth Press, 52 Tavistock Square, London, W.C.1 1937

WORLD-MAKERS & WORLD-SHAKERS SERIES
§ Brown cloth printed in black. Yellow dust wrapper printed in green.
79 pp. (5) $7\frac{1}{4}$ x $4\frac{3}{4}$.
Published June 1937; **5,000 copies printed.**

418. **Sackville-West, V.** *Joan of Arc* Published by Leonard and Virginia Woolf at The Hogarth Press, 52 Tavistock Square, London, W.C.1 1937

WORLD-MAKERS & WORLD-SHAKERS SERIES
§ Brown cloth printed in black. Yellow dust wrapper printed in green.
80 pp. (5) $7\frac{1}{4}$ x $4\frac{3}{4}$.
Published June 1937; **5,000 copies printed.**

419. **Sackville-West, V.** *Pepita* Published by Leonard and Virginia Woolf at the Hogarth Press, 52 Tavistock Square, London, W.C. 1937

§ Brown cloth printed in gilt. Cream dust wrapper printed in black.
282 pp. (2) $8\frac{5}{8}$ x $5\frac{1}{2}$.
Published October 1937; **9,950 copies printed.**

420. **Sharpe, Ella Freeman** *Dream Analysis A Practical Handbook for Psycho-Analysts* Published by Leonard and Virginia Woolf at The Hogarth Press, Tavistock Square, London and The Institute of Psycho-Analysis 1937

THE INTERNATIONAL PSYCHO-ANALYTICAL LIBRARY NO. 29
§ Green cloth printed in gilt. Dust wrapper not seen.
211 pp. (5) $8\frac{3}{4}$ x $5\frac{1}{2}$.
Published November 1937; 1,020 copies printed.

421. **Strachey, Marjorie** *Mazzini, Garibaldi & Cavour* Published by Leonard and Virginia Woolf at The Hogarth Press, 52 Tavistock Square, London W.C.1 1937

WORLD-MAKERS & WORLD-SHAKERS SERIES
§ Brown cloth printed in black. Yellow dust wrapper printed in green.
80 pp. (5) $7\frac{1}{4}$ x $4\frac{3}{4}$.
Published June 1937; **5,050 copies printed.**

422. **Tree, Viola** *Can I Help You?* *Your Manners--Menus--Amusements--Friends--Charades--Make-Ups--Travel--Calling--Children--Love Affairs* Illustrated by Virginia Parsons. Published by Leonard and Virginia Woolf at The Hogarth Press, 52 Tavistock Square, London, W.C. 1937
§ Blue cloth printed in gilt. Orange dust wrapper printed in red.
256 pp. (5) $8\frac{5}{8}$ x $5\frac{1}{2}$.
Published October 1937; 2,038 copies printed.

423. **Woolf, Virginia** *The Years* Published by Leonard and Virginia Woolf at The Hogarth Press, Tavistock Square, London 1937
§ Pale green cloth printed in gilt. Cream dust wrapper printed in black and brown.
469 pp. (2) $7\frac{1}{8}$ x $4\frac{3}{4}$.
Published March 1937; 18,142 copies printed.

1938

424. **Allott, Kenneth** *Poems* The Hogarth Press 52 Tavistock Square, London, W.C.1 1938
§ Grey cloth printed in red. Grey dust wrapper printed in red.
64 pp. (8) $8\frac{5}{8}$ x $5\frac{1}{2}$.
Published October 1938; number of copies not known.

425. **Arnold, Percy** *The Bankers of London* The Hogarth Press 52 Tavistock Square, London, W.C.1 1938
§ Blue cloth printed in black. Cream dust wrapper printed in blue.
108 pp. (5) $7\frac{3}{8}$ x $4\frac{3}{4}$.
Published November 1938; 1,200 copies printed.

426. **Bell, Quentin, Editor** *Julian Bell Essays, Poems and Letters* With contributions by J. M. Keynes, David Garnett, Charles Mauron, C. Day Lewis and E. M. Forster The Hogarth Press 52 Tavistock Square, London, W.C.1 1938
§ Blue cloth printed in gilt. Cream dust wrapper printed in black.
396 pp. (8) $8\frac{3}{4}$ x $5\frac{1}{2}$.
Published November 1938; 1,200 printed (600 pulped).
NOTE: Julian Bell, Virginia Woolf's nephew, was killed in 1937 while serving as an ambulance driver in Spain.

427. **Benedict, Libby** *The Refugees* Published by Leonard and Virginia Woolf at The Hogarth Press, 52 Tavistock Square, London, W.C.1 1938
§ Blue cloth printed in black. Buff dust wrapper printed in red and black.
344 pp. (5) $7\frac{3}{8}$ x $4\frac{3}{4}$.
Published March 1938; 1,222 copies printed.

428. **Cole, G. D. H.** *The Machinery of Socialist Planning* **The** Hogarth Press 52 Tavistock Square, London, W.C.1 1938
§ Green cloth wrappers printed in black.
80 pp. (5) $7\frac{1}{4}$ x $4\frac{3}{4}$.
Month of publication not known; 1,500 copies printed.

429. **Cole, Margaret** *Books and the People* The Hogarth Press 52 Tavistock Square, London, W.C.1 1938
DAY TO DAY PAMPHLETS NO. 38
§ Green paper wrappers printed in blue.
48 pp. (5) $7\frac{1}{4}$ x $4\frac{3}{4}$.
Published October 1938; 1,550 copies printed.

430. **Dutt, R. Palme** *The Political and Social Doctrine of Communism* The Hogarth Press 52 Tavistock Square, London, W.C.1 1938
DAY TO DAY PAMPHLETS NO. 39
§ Red paper wrappers printed in black.
44 pp. (5) $7\frac{1}{4}$ x $4\frac{3}{4}$.
Published October 1938; number of copies not known.

431. **Isherwood, Christopher** *Lions and Shadows An Education in the Twenties* Published by Leonard & Virginia Woolf at The Hogarth Press, 52 Tavistock Square, London, W.C.1 1938
§ Blue cloth printed in black. Grey dust wrapper printed in brown.
312 pp. (5) $7\frac{1}{4}$ x $4\frac{3}{4}$.
Published March 1938; 3,580 copies printed.

432. **Laforgue, Dr. René**   *Clinical Aspects of Psycho-Analysis*
Translated from the French by Joan Hall. Published by
Leonard and Virginia Woolf at The Hogarth Press, 52
Tavistock Square, London, and The Institute of Psycho-
Analysis 1938
THE INTERNATIONAL PSYCHO-ANALYTICAL LIBRARY NO. 31
§ Green cloth printed in gilt. Dust wrapper not seen.
300 pp. (5) $8\frac{3}{4}$ x $5\frac{1}{2}$.
Published May 1938; 960 copies printed.
NOTE: The last book published by the Hogarth Press to have the
Woolf's name on the title page.

433. **Lehmann, John**   *New Writing*   New Series I, Autumn
1938. Edited by John Lehmann with the assistance of
Christopher Isherwood (&) Stephen Spender. The Ho-
garth Press 52 Tavistock Square London, W.C.1
§ Yellow cloth printed in blue.   White dust wrapper
printed in blue and green.
240 pp. (7) $8\frac{3}{4}$ x $5\frac{5}{8}$.
Published November 1938; number of copies not known.
NOTE: Volumes 1 & 2 of the original series were published by
John Lane; volumes 3 to 5 by Lawrence & Wishart.

434. **Macaulay, Rose**   *The Writings of E. M. Forster* Published
by Leonard & Virginia Woolf at The Hogarth Press,
52 Tavistock Square, London, W.C.1 1938
§ Blue cloth printed in black.   Light pink dust wrapper
printed in dark pink.
304 pp. (5) $7\frac{1}{4}$ x $4\frac{3}{4}$.
Published March 1938; 2,250 copies printed (1,065 of
these were supplied to Harcourt, Brace for the American
edition).

435. **Nott, Kathleen**   *Mile End*   The Hogarth Press 52
Tavistock Square, London, W.C.1 1938
§ Grey cloth printed in red. White dust wrapper printed
in blue.
510 pp. (5) $7\frac{3}{8}$ x $4\frac{7}{8}$.
Published October 1938; 1,200 copies printed.

436. **Origo, Iris** *Tribune of Rome   A Biography of Cola di Rienzo*
The Hogarth Press 52 Tavistock Square, London, W.C.1
1938
§ Black cloth printed in gilt.   Yellow dust wrapper
printed in black.
265 pp. (5) $8\frac{5}{8}$ x $5\frac{1}{2}$.
Publication date and number of copies printed not known.

437. **Rilke, Rainer Maria** *Later Poems*   Translated from the
German with an Introduction and Commentary by J. B.
Leishman.   The Hogarth Press   52 Tavistock Square
London, W.C.1 1938
§ Orange-brown cloth printed in gilt. Dust wrapper not
seen.
277 pp. (5) $8\frac{1}{4}$ x $5\frac{1}{4}$.
Published May 1938; 1,020 copies printed.

438A. **Sackville-West, V.** *Solitude   A Poem* The Hogarth Press
52 Tavistock Square, London, W.C.1 1938
§ Dark orange cloth; vellum spine printed in gilt. White
dust wrapper printed in black.
56 pp. (2) $8\frac{7}{8}$ x $5\frac{3}{4}$.
Published November 1938; limited to 100 numbered and
signed copies.
NOTE: First (limited) edition.

438B. **Sackville-West, V.** *Solitude   A Poem* The Hogarth Press
52 Tavistock Square, London, W.C.1 1938
§ Orange cloth printed in gilt. Cream dust wrapper
printed in black.
56 pp. (2) $8\frac{3}{4}$ x $5\frac{1}{2}$.
Published November 1938; 3,018 copies printed.
NOTE: First (trade) edition.

439. **Upward, Edward**   *Journey to the Border*   Published by
Leonard and Virginia Woolf at The Hogarth Press, 52
Tavistock Square, London, W.C. 1938
§ Blue cloth printed in black. Light pink dust wrapper
printed in red.
256 pp. (5) $7\frac{1}{4}$ x $4\frac{1}{2}$.
Published March 1938; number of copies not known.

440. **Woolf, Virginia** *Three Guineas* The Hogarth Press 52
Tavistock Square, London, W.C.1 1938
§ Yellow cloth printed in gilt. Cream dust wrapper
printed in mauve and blue.
329 pp. (5) $7\frac{1}{4}$ x $4\frac{3}{4}$.
Published June 1938; 16,250 copies printed.

Appendix I
THE SERIES

THE HOGARTH ESSAYS

The
Revival of Æsthetics

HUBERT WALEY

THE HOGARTH PRESS

THE HOGARTH ESSAYS
FIRST SERIES

NOTE: The volumes in this series vary slightly in size.

THE HOGARTH ESSAYS

SECOND SERIES

HOGARTH LECTURES
No. 15

POETRY IN FRANCE
AND ENGLAND

JEAN STEWART

Miss Stewart traces the evolution of poetry in the two countries, showing how, at certain periods, the guiding principles
of the art were similar in both countries, although the appli-
cation of the principles was characteristically different, and
how, at other times, each country follows an entirely independent line of development.

THE HOGARTH PRESS

THE HOGARTH LECTURES ON LITERATURE
FIRST SERIES

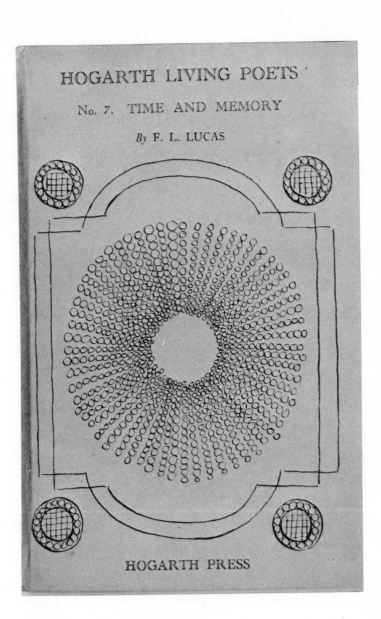

HOGARTH LIVING POETS

No. 7.   TIME AND MEMORY

By F. L. LUCAS

HOGARTH PRESS

HOGARTH LIVING POETS

FIRST SERIES

HOGARTH LIVING POETS
SECOND SERIES

HOGARTH STORIES

1927

MERTTENS LECTURES ON WAR AND PEACE

DAY TO DAY PAMPHLETS

No. 5

PROTECTION AND FREE TRADE

By L. M. FRASER

THE HOGARTH PRESS

One Shilling & Sixpence net

DAY TO DAY PAMPHLETS

DAY TO DAY PAMPHLETS

(*Cont'd*)

BIOGRAPHIES THROUGH THE EYES OF CONTEMPORARIES SERIES

1934

1. Edmund Blunden, Compiler, *Charles Lamb   His Life
   Recorded by his Contemporaries*   (337)

1935

2. E. M. Delafield, Compiler, *The Brontes   Their Lives
   Recorded by their Contemporaries*   (366)

WORLD-MAKERS AND WORLD-SHAKERS SERIES

1937

1. V. Sackville-West, *Joan of Arc*   (418)
2. Naomi Mitchison & R. H. S. Crossman, *Socrates*   (415)
3. Marjorie Strachey, *Mazzini, Garibaldi and Cavour*   (421)
4. L. B. Pekin, *Darwin*   (417)

PSYCHO-ANALYTICAL EPITOMES

1937

1. Sigmund Freud, *A General Selection from the Works
   of Sigmund Freud*   (409)
2 Melanie Klein & Joan Riviere, *Love, Hate and
   Reparation*   (412)

1939

3. Roger Money-Kyrle, *Superstition and Society*
4. Sigmund Freud, *Civilization, War and Death*

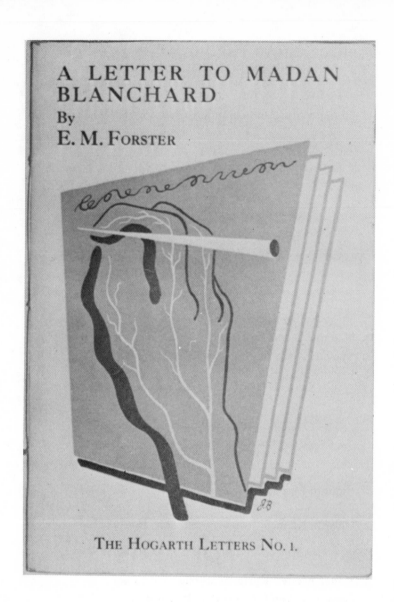

A LETTER TO MADAN
BLANCHARD
By
E. M. FORSTER

THE HOGARTH LETTERS NO. 1.

THE HOGARTH LETTERS

NOTE: 500 sets of sheets of each volume, with the exception of no. 7, were bound and issued in one volume in 1933

THE INTERNATIONAL PSYCHO-ANALYTICAL LIBRARY

1921

1. J. J. Putnam, *Addresses on Psycho-Analysis*
2. Sandor Ferenczi, *Psycho-Analysis and the War Neuroses*
3. J. C. Flugel, *The Psycho-Analytic Study of the Family*

1922

NOTE: The Hogarth Press took over The International Psycho-Analytical Library in 1922; the Hogarth imprint appears on the cover and dust wrapper beginning with no. 4, but it does not appear on the title page until no. 8.

4. Sigmund Freud, *Beyond the Pleasure Principle* (21)
6. Sigmund Freud, *Group Psychology and the Analysis of the Ego* (22)

1923

5. Ernest Jones, *Essays in Applied Psycho-Analysis* (34)

1924-1925

7. - 10. Sigmund Freud, *Collected Papers* 4 vols. (44)

1926

11. Sandor Ferenczi, *Further Contributions to the Theory and Technique of Psycho-Analysis* (89)

1927

12. Sigmund Freud, *The Ego and the Id* (119)
13. Karl Abraham, *Selected Papers of Karl Abraham* (114)

1928

14. John Rickman, *Index Psychoanalyticus 1893-1926* (172)
15. Sigmund Freud, *The Future of an Illusion* (163)

1930

16. Roger Money-Kyrle, *The Meaning of Sacrifice* (229)
17. Sigmund Freud, *Civilization and its Discontents* (223)
18. J. C. Flugel, *The Psychology of Clothes* (221)

1931

19. Theodor Reik, *Ritual Psycho-Analytic Studies* (267)
20. Ernest Jones, *On the Nightmare* (260)

THE INTERNATIONAL PSYCHO-ANALYTICAL
LIBRARY

(Cont'd)

1932

NOTE: This series is still continuing.

Appendix II
BOOKS
HANDPRINTED
BY LEONARD &
VIRGINIA WOOLF

BOOKS HANDPRINTED BY
LEONARD AND VIRGINIA WOOLF

1917
Virginia & L. S. Woolf, *Two Stories*   **(1)**

1918
Katherine Mansfield, *Prelude*   **(2)**
C. N. Sidney Woolf, *Poems*   **(3)**

1919
T. S. Eliot, *Poems*   **(4)**
Hope Mirrlees, *Paris a Poem*   **(5)**
J. Middleton Murry, *The Critic in Judgment*   **(6)**
Virginia Woolf, *Kew Gardens*   **(7)**

1920
E. M. Forster, *The Story of the Siren*   **(9)**

1921
Clive Bell, *Poems*   **(12)**
Roger Fry, *Twelve Original Woodcuts*   **(13)**
Frank Prewett, *Poems*   **(15)**
Leonard Woolf, *Stories of the East*   **(16)**

1922
Ruth Manning-Sanders, *Karn*   **(23)**
Fredegond Shove, *Daybreak*   **(24)**

1923
Clive Bell, *The Legend of Monte Della Sibilla*   **(27)**
T. S. Eliot, *The Waste Land*   **(28)**
E. M. Forster, *Pharos and Pharillon*   **(29)**
Robert Graves, *The Feather Bed*   **(33)**
Ena Limebeer, *To a Proud Phantom*   **(35)**
Herbert Read, *Mutations of the Phoenix*   **(38)**

1924
Theodora Bosanquet, *Henry James at Work*   **(42)**
John Crowe Ransom, *Grace After Meat*   **(51)**

BOOKS HANDPRINTED BY
LEONARD AND VIRGINIA WOOLF

(Cont'd)

Appendix III
KEY TO PRINTERS

KEY TO PRINTERS

1 Handprinted by the Woolfs
2 R & R Clark
3 Neill & Co.
4 Cranach Press, Weimar
5 Garden City Press
6 Printed in the U. S. A.
7 Western Printing
8 Hazell, Watson & Viney
9 Alcuin Press
10 Pelican Press
11 The Prompt Press
12 Wm. Clowes & Sons
13 Printer not known
14 Richard Madley
15 Printed in Germany
16 A. A. Tanner & Son
17 Purnell & Sons
18 Herbert Reiach
19 Billing & Sons
20 Leagrave Press
21 Star and Gazette Co.
22 Loxley Bros. Ltd.
23 Lowe & Brydone Printers Ltd.
24 T. and A. Constable
25 Vacher & Sons, Ltd.
26 The Society for Graphic Industry, Vienna
27 C. Fromme, Vienna
28 K. Liebel, Vienna
29 Spamer, Leipzig
30 The Hereford Times Ltd.
31 The Leicester Co-operative Printing Society Ltd.
32 The Complete Press

Appendix IV
HOGARTH GHOSTS

HOGARTH GHOSTS

Books announced for publication or as
published but which never appeared.

1. Walter De La Mare, *Atmosphere in Fiction*   **1927**

   Announced as published in The Hogarth Essays Series on the dust
   wrapper of William Plomer's *I Speak of Africa.*

2. Peter Quennell, *Revolutions in Literary Method*   **1931**

   Announced as in preparation in The Hogarth Lectures on Literature
   Series in Norman MacLeod's *German Lyric Poetry.*

3. Hugh Walpole, *The Historical Novel*   **1930**

   Announced as in preparation in The Hogarth Lectures on Literature
   Series in Sir Arthur Quiller-Couch's *A Lecture on Lectures.*

4. Virginia Woolf, *Poetry, Fiction & the Future*   **1927**

   Announced as published in The Hogarth Essays Series on the dust
   wrapper of William Plomer's *I Speak of Africa.* First published in the
   New York Herald Tribune, 14 and 21 August 1927, and later published under the title "The Narrow Bridge of Art" in *Granite and
   Rainbow.*

5. Virginia Woolf, *Phases of Fiction*   **1928**

   Announced as in preparation in The Hogarth Lectures on Literature
   Series in Sir Arthur Quiller-Couch's *A Lecture on Lectures.* First published in the Bookman, April, May, and June 1929, and later published
   in *Granite and Rainbow.*

Index

INDEX